FoL
2

RODALE'S
SUCCESSFUL ORGANIC GARDENING®
COMPANION
PLANTING

RODALE'S
SUCCESSFUL ORGANIC GARDENING®
COMPANION
PLANTING

TEXT BY SUSAN McCLURE

PLANT BY PLANT GUIDE BY SALLY ROTH

Rodale Press, Emmaus, Pennsylvania

Our Mission

We publish books that empower people's lives.

RODALE BOOKS

If you have any questions or comments concerning this book, please write to:

Rodale Press
Book Readers' Service
33 East Minor Street
Emmaus, PA 18098

Library of Congress Cataloging-in-Publication Data

McClure, Susan.
   Companion planting / text by Susan McClure ; plant by plant guide by Sally Roth
      p.   cm. — (Rodale's successful organic gardening)
   Includes index.
   ISBN 0–87596–615–2 hardcover — ISBN 0–87596–616–0 paperback
     1. Companion planting. 2. Companion crops. 3. Plants, Useful.
4. Organic gardening. I. Roth, Sally. II. Title. III. Series.
SB453.6.M38 1994
635'.048—dc20   93–44918
                          CIP

Printed in the United States of America on acid-free ∞, recycled paper ♻

Rodale Press Staff:
   Executive Editor: Margaret Lydic Balitas
   Managing Editor: Barbara W. Ellis
   Editor: Nancy J. Ondra
   Copy Editor: Carolyn R. Mandarano

Produced for Rodale Press by Weldon Russell Pty Ltd
107 Union Street, North Sydney NSW 2060, Australia
a member of the Weldon International Group of Companies

   Publisher: Elaine Russell
   Publishing Manager: Susan Hurley
   Managing Editor: Ariana Klepac
   Assistant Editor: Libby Frederico
   Horticultural Consultant: Cheryl Maddocks
   Copy Editor: Yani Silvana
   Designer: Rowena Sheppard
   Picture Researcher: Anne Ferrier
   Illustrators: Barbara Rodanska, Jan Smith
   Macintosh Layout Artist: Edwina Ryan
   Indexer: Michael Wyatt
   Production Manager: Dianne Leddy

A KEVIN WELDON PRODUCTION

Distributed in the book trade by St. Martin's Press

4 6 8 10 9 7 5   hardcover
2 4 6 8 10 9 7 5 3   paperback

Opposite: 'Rodeo' red cabbage

Half title: Flowering chives

Opposite title page: 'Halloween' pumpkins

Title page: 'Hidcote' lavender

Opposite contents: 'Sensation' cosmos

Contents: 'Master Robert' dahlia (top left)

Back cover: 'Dee Prince' chrysanthemum (top); nasturtiums with ruby chard (center)

CONTENTS

INTRODUCTION

When you try companion planting, you're using a centuries-old technique that gardeners have relied on for controlling pests and improving the harvest. Some of the earliest known experiments with companion planting were recorded by writers like Theophrastus (300 B.C.), Pliny (50 A.D.), and John Gerard (1597 A.D.). These and other early writers chronicled mankind's experimentation with useful plants in natural histories, herbals, and books for physicians and gardeners. In addition to writing about plants that can serve people, they left notes on the ways that two or more plants could benefit or harm each other's growth. These observations were essential for early gardeners who couldn't stop by their local garden center to pick up a bottle of soap spray or a box of pheromone traps. They had to rely on more natural means to make a garden grow. Now, modern gardeners are also beginning to appreciate the value and safety of using companion planting as a basis for garden pest control.

Today, gardeners who try companion planting are using methods based on historical and contemporary gardening folklore. While much of this folklore has not been substantiated, some scientists are working to test and document how different plants interact with each other and the world around them. Some of the most interesting research has centered on the different ways that plants can defend themselves against pests. Some plants stockpile bitter compounds in their leaves after being chewed on, and these flavorings may be repellent enough to inspire the pest to move on to another plant. Other plants are endowed with natural insecticides that are unhealthy for the pest that chews or sucks on the plant, but not for beneficial insects. Still others manufacture hormones that resemble natural insect hormones closely enough to stop normal development.

Repelling pests is just one aspect of companion planting—attracting beneficial insects is another. Many plants attract nectar- and pollen-eating insects, which pollinate their flowers and help them set fruits and seeds. As a bonus, some of these nectar- and pollen-eaters—like lacewings and hover flies—produce larvae that attack plant-eating insects. The plants that lure these beneficial insects to your garden develop a small army that helps defend your plantings against pests.

As you read on, you'll learn more about the many wonderful ways plants have adapted to their particular environments and pest problems. And you'll discover how you can use these adaptations to plan effective companion plantings for your own garden. Some of this information is based on years of gardening folklore; some of it is based on hard research. *Rodale's Successful Organic Gardening: Companion Planting* will present you with both perspectives. Use the techniques presented in this book to improve your existing garden or to start a new garden. We hope you'll try companion planting, a legacy centuries old, to have the best modern organic garden possible.

A key part of successful companion planting is increasing the diversity of your garden plantings. Mixtures of flowers, vegetables, and herbs can attract a wide variety of beneficial insects, and they look beautiful as well.

How to Use This Book

Wouldn't it be great if you could just plant your garden and forget it? Your plants would grow lush and healthy—without you adding lots of fertilizer or worrying about pest problems. Well, any kind of garden will need some care, but you *can* encourage your plants to work together, sharing water and nutrients and protecting each other from pesky insects. That's what *Rodale's Successful Organic Gardening: Companion Planting* is all about.

The chapters that follow will tell you all you need to know to get a good start with companion planting. You'll find out how it works and what it can do for your garden. You'll discover the different ways companion plants can repel pests, attract beneficial insects, and encourage or discourage the growth of other plants. You'll learn what kind of groundwork you need to provide to give the plants a healthy start so they can fulfill your expectations. And you'll see what it takes to care for companions through the season so you'll have the best harvest ever.

"Companion Planting Basics," starting on page 12, gives you some insight into how the technique works. Companion planting is based on sound principles like encouraging diversity and using qualities your plants already have, such as the ability to repel pests or fix nitrogen. You'll also find that some plants can be helpful for nearby companions, while others can actually discourage growth.

"Companion Planting for Pest Control," starting on page 22, will teach you how to minimize pest damage without using pesticides. Simply by organizing the right network of companions, you can deter, trap, or confuse pests. You'll learn about the powerful allies in a companion garden—plants that can repel or kill pests.

You'll also meet enticing plants—flowers that are sure to attract a bevy of beneficial insects. You'll discover which weeds can harbor harmful insects and diseases and which can make useful companion plants. Once you've planned a strategy for limiting garden pests, you can look forward to a more carefree growing season.

"Interplanting," starting on page 34, will help you find the most effective plant groupings so your companions will be compatible, not competitive. Interplanting allows you to blend many plants that will share garden resources. You'll learn how to plan the most effective garden groupings by considering each plant's habits and needs.

Once you know what you want to grow, it's time to generate a comprehensive garden plan. Flip to "Creating a Planting Plan," starting on page 50, to find out how to take a systematic approach to garden planning. Add in crop rotation, a vital system for cycling crops to different parts of the garden season after season. Crop rotation makes the most of soil fertility and minimizes garden pests. Use what you've learned to sketch out plans for early-season, midseason, and late-season planting.

When the growing season arrives, you'll have a chance to turn your garden into a living laboratory. See "Planting Companions," starting on page 64, to find out how to get your crops off to the best start possible. Learn how to prepare a rich organic soil that will provide ideal growing conditions. Develop a diversity of different planting areas, including raised beds and single, double, or wide rows. Then pick a spacing system that will let you get the most from each planting area.

Keep the garden on track all season by referring to "Caring for Companions," starting on page 74. Find out when and how to water most efficiently. See why you should mulch to make the garden grow better with less work. If your plants need a nutrient boost, learn which fertilizer does the best job and how to apply it. Nutrient-rich compost is one possibility, and you'll learn to make your own from a blend of garden wastes and kitchen scraps. You'll also learn how to treat pest and disease problems organically.

Finally, you are ready to reap your reward. Be sure to harvest edible crops at just the right time, when they are ripe, tender, and delicious. You'll find out how to produce edibles extra early or late—and how to extend the growing season with protective structures and cold-tolerant crops. And you'll learn why and how to clean up the garden at the end of the season. Then you'll be ready to begin a new garden for next year.

Plant by Plant Guide

As you plan your companion garden, you'll want a source for suggestions of just what companions work best for particular crops. You'll find that information in the "Plant by Plant Guide," starting on page 94. There are individual entries for over 100 different crops and companions, arranged alphabetically by common name. Each entry explores allies that improve growth or flavor, companions that share space well, plant enemies, growing guidelines, and special tips gleaned from folklore and scientific studies. The diagram below helps explain what to look for on these practical pages.

Use the information in these entries as a starting point for your planning. Keep track of which suggestions work for you to fine-tune your companion planting plans.

Sample page from the "Plant by Plant Guide."

COMPANION PLANTING BASICS

When you discuss the subject of companion planting, it can be hard to separate the fact from the fiction. The advice that's thrown about sounds good enough for tabloid headlines: "Miracle Marigolds Keep Tomatoes Pest-Free," or "Powerful Plant Sends Moles Packing." In this chapter, you'll learn how to tell if these recommendations are based on fact or if they are too good to be true. You'll find out that plants actually *can* affect each other for good or ill. You'll learn the basics of *why* companion planting works and how you can use it to make your landscape and garden grow better, yield more, and have less pest problems.

Many of the combinations you'll read about are based on folklore: Gardeners swear that they work, but scientists haven't been able to verify it. In some cases, though, science *has* been able to explain why certain combinations work well together. For instance, American settlers described how native American Indians interplanted pole beans with corn. The most obvious reason for this combination's success was that the strength of the fibrous corn stalks supported the twining beans. Research now tells us about the additional benefits of this combination. *Rhizobium* bacteria colonies on the bean roots capture atmospheric nitrogen for the legume. Some of the nitrogen is released into the soil, replenishing nutrients used by both the corn and bean crops.

Your garden can benefit from the many years of observation and research that have gone into modern-day companion planting recommendations. This chapter will help you decide where to begin. "What Is Companion Planting?" on page 14 explains how companion planting differs from other kinds of planting, including its advantages and disadvantages. "How Does Companion Planting Work?" on page 16 tells about the various ways companions can benefit neighboring plants and discourage pests. "Getting Started with Companions" on page 18 covers the basics of trying and evaluating companion planting techniques in your own garden. And "Plant Antagonists" on page 20 tells why some plants just don't get along and what that means for you and your crops.

Some garden plants can actually improve the soil where they grow. Legumes, including plants like peas, beans, clover, and lupines, work with beneficial bacteria to trap nitrogen from the air and use it for good growth.

What Is Companion Planting?

In the simplest terms, companion planting is the technique of combining two plants for a particular purpose (usually pest control). In practice, though, you'll find that there are many different factors that influence how plants work together as companions. For instance, if your crops are regularly attacked by insects, you can use companions to hide, repel, or trap pests. Other companions provide food and shelter to attract and protect beneficial insects. And some plants grow well together just because they don't compete for light or rooting space. The sections below cover some of the most dependable functions of companion plants.

The aroma of garlic and onions is a powerful deterrent to many pests.

Repelling with Smells

Many insects use their sense of smell to find their way to favored crops. Imported cabbageworms, for instance, are attracted to the mustard oils in their favored host plants. Onion maggots are lured to your onions by the sulfur compounds the crop releases.

One way to use companion planting to protect your plants is to mask their odors with other powerful smells. Plants like garlic, for instance, release deterrent aromas into the air that may chase away insects such as bean beetles and potato bugs; onions can prevent pests from attacking strawberries or tomatoes. Mint may keep cabbage loopers off cabbage plants, while basil can discourage tomato hornworms on tomatoes. The smell of tomato foliage (which contains solanine, a poisonous and volatile compound) can deter cabbage loopers from nearby cabbage and broccoli plants.

Try pungent plants as an edging around garden beds or mix them in among your crops. Or, if you can't grow the repellents close enough to your crops, try spreading clippings of the scented plants over garden beds for the same effect. To learn more about the ways companion plants can repel pests from your crops, see "How Plants Control Pests" on page 24.

Luring Pests from Crops

Some plants have an almost irresistible appeal for certain pests. Nasturtiums, for instance, are an excellent attractant plant because they're a favorite of aphids. Colorado potato beetles find black nightshade (*Solanum nigrum*) more alluring than even your best potato plants.

Attractant plants can protect your crops in two ways. First, they act as decoys to lure pests away from

Besides producing pretty (and edible) flowers, nasturtiums may lure aphids from your crops.

For a great strawberry crop, try interplanting with onions for pest control and borage for vigorous growth.

your desirable crops. Second, they make it easier to control the pests since the insects are concentrated on a few plants. Once pests are "trapped," you can either pull out the attractant plants and destroy them along with the pests or apply some other type of control measure to the infested plants. To learn more about choosing and using attractant plants, see "Decoy and Trap Crops" on page 32.

Sheltering Beneficial Insects

Not all insects are garden enemies. Many actually help your garden grow by eating or parasitizing plant pests. You can encourage these beneficial creatures to make a home in your garden by planting their favorite flowering plants. Growing dill, for example, can attract

pest-eating spiders, lacewings, and parasitic wasps, which will help control caterpillars on cabbage, beetles on cucumbers, and aphids on lettuce. "Companions as Nursery Crops" on page 28 offers more detailed information on selecting and planting nursery crops.

Combining Complementary Crops

Some plants make ideal garden companions simply because they don't compete, even when planted close together in small spaces. Plants like deep-rooted squash and shallow-rooted onions occupy different soil zones, so their roots can draw on different nutrient sources. Crops that need lots of nutrients (heavy feeders, like cabbage, corn, eggplant, and squash) combine well with light feeders, like garlic and beans. Taller crops like corn, trellised beans, and sunflowers can provide welcome light

Flat, daisy-like flowers are a good source of pollen and nectar for a variety of beneficial insects.

shade for ground-hugging cucumbers and lettuce.

Besides making more efficient use of space, mixing crops with compatible growth habits also increases the diversity in your garden. This, in turn, makes it harder for some pests to find and move between your plants. You'll find more details on planning complementary combinations in "Interplanting," starting on page 34.

Beneficial insects are also attracted to mixed plantings, since they can find plenty of food and shelter. Plus, mixing flowering and fruiting crops can give you a garden that's attractive as well as productive.

Lettuce and sunflowers can be good garden companions. The low-growing lettuce acts as a living mulch to keep the soil moist, while tall sunflowers to the south or west provide light shade for this heat-sensitive salad crop.

Besides being edible crops, flowering plants like strawberries and chives can attract beneficial insects.

How Does Companion Planting Work?

When you arrange your garden according to the principles of companion planting, you combine plants that can share resources—water, light, and nutrients—and take advantage of the natural defenses plants use to protect themselves from pests, diseases, and other plants. Increasing the diversity of your garden plantings and incorporating plants with particularly useful characteristics are both part of successful companion planting.

Creating Diversity

In contrast to the wide diversity of natural systems—like forests and prairies—our gardens and farms tend to contain neat, identical plantings of just a few different plant species. These large groups of similar plants, called monocultures, are prime targets for insect and disease attack. For instance, one study found that cucumber monocultures attracted 10 to 30 times more disease-carrying striped cucumber beetles than mixed plantings. Increasing the diversity of your garden plantings is a natural and effective way to minimize pest and disease problems.

Technically, adding diversity could be as simple as increasing the number of different plants in your garden. Sounds simple—until you realize that you have a limited amount of room in your garden, which is taken up by your favorite crops. But if you create

Clover, peas, and other legumes can enrich the soil for nearby crops.

a *planned* diversity, you can still have good (or even better) yields from the same amount of space. Instead of growing the same vegetable cultivars in the same beds every year, try changing their positions each year or at least try different cultivars; see "Planning Crop Rotations" on page 54 for more information on this technique. To get even more diversity, try open-pollinated seeds instead of hybrids. The plants from open-pollinated seed are all just a little different genetically, so even if pests or diseases attack some of the plants, the rest of the crop may be spared.

An easy and pleasant way to add diversity to the vegetable garden is to add a variety of flowering plants. Mix annual flowers and herbs in the beds or rows of vegetables, or create permanent beds nearby for flowering perennials, shrubs, vines, and bulbs. Besides looking good, the flowers provide a source of food and shelter for spiders and beneficial insects that eat or parasitize plant pests. Start with early spring bulbs and wildflowers, add late spring- and summer-blooming perennials, annuals, shrubs, and herbs, and follow with fall asters and other late bloomers to attract and protect beneficials all season long.

Pretty flowering perennials can help attract honeybees, promoting good pollination of fruit and vegetable crops.

Enriching the Soil

All plants withdraw some nutrients from the soil as they grow, but some actually return more nutrients than they consume. Legumes—plants like peas, beans, and clover—have a mutually beneficial relationship with nitrogen-fixing *Rhizobium* bacteria. These bacteria colonize legume roots, absorbing up to 20 percent of the sugars the plants produce. The bacteria use this energy to capture atmospheric nitrogen (nitrogen gas) and convert it into nitrogen compounds that plants can use.

Not all plants make good companions. Although this combination looks nice, the nasturtiums may attract flea beetles, and the marigolds can inhibit the growth of the cabbage.

Some of this nitrogen goes directly back to the host plant. A few long-season legumes, like pole lima beans, chickpeas, peanuts, and yard-long beans, can produce all the nitrogen they need. Quicker-cropping peas, bush lima beans, and snap beans get about half of their total nitrogen needs from the bacteria.

Another part of the nitrogen trapped by the *Rhizobium* bacteria is released into the soil as the nodule-bearing roots die off and decompose. This nitrogen is available during the season to boost the growth of any companion plants growing nearby. The big bonus comes when you turn the foliage and roots of the legumes into the soil. When they decay, they can release enough nitrogen to feed the next crop you grow.

Affecting Insect Behavior

A key part of creating effective crop combinations is employing your plants' natural abilities to attract, confuse, or deter insects. Some plants produce repellent or toxic compounds that chase pests away or stop them from feeding. For instance, one wild Florida mint smells so intensely that only one pest will eat it: a caterpillar that feeds on the leaves and regurgitates the residue onto himself to scare away his predators. In some cases, the aromatic compounds released by plants can mask the scent of interplanted companion crops. Summer savory, for example, may help hide your bush beans from pests, while tansy is said to repel Colorado potato beetles from a potato planting. For a more detailed explanation of how plants can chase pests away, see "Companions as Repellents" on page 26.

Other plants have the power to attract insects. Why would you want to draw insects *into* your garden? First of all, trap and decoy crops can lure pests away from your other plants, reducing or preventing damage to your harvest. (Plus, it's easiest to spot and control pests when they have congregated on a few particular plants.) Second, it's smart to attract lacewings, hover flies, and other beneficial insects to your garden so they can control some of the pest species for you. Plants that produce large quantities of easily accessible pollen and nectar—like yarrow, fennel, and goldenrod—provide shelter and supplemental food for hungry beneficials. "Companions as Nursery Crops" on page 28 and "Decoy and Trap Crops" on page 32 offer more information on the ways attractant plants can benefit your garden crops. With careful planning on your part, plants can protect each other from many pests.

Plants like goldenrod, dill, and yarrow attract beneficials with ample quantities of pollen and nectar.

Getting Started with Companions

The amount of satisfaction and success you get from companion planting depends on how much effort you put into it. Even some of the most basic principles, like increasing diversity and rotating crops, can bring excellent results. But to get the most benefits, you need to be willing to do some planning and experimenting. Enjoy your successes, learn from the failures, and keep an open mind—these are the keys to successful companion planting.

Picking Potential Companions

With so many possible combinations, it can be hard to know where to start. To increase your chances of success, try a companion planting scheme that has been found effective in scientific studies or has the confirmation of a wide variety of gardeners from varying climates. (Many of these combinations are suggested throughout this book.) As you gain confidence, you can branch out to try less-proven companion combinations, or make up your own.

You might want to start by selecting a companion for one of your favorite crops—tomatoes, for example. If you look up the Tomato entry in the "Plant by Plant Guide," starting on page 94, you'll find recommendations for allies and compatible companions, as well as helpful growing information. Use these suggestions as a basis for your trials.

Also keep your eyes open for existing garden plants that you can use in your own companion planting experiments. Look closely at flowers around your yard to see which harbor a wealth of beneficial insects; you may want to plant more of these attractant plants. If you find a quick-

Don't forget to try out companions in the flower garden, too!

Interplant crops with lemon balm and other herbs, or grow herbs in containers and move as needed for pest control.

growing weed or vegetable that is crawling with a bumper crop of pests, take note—it could make a good trap crop to lure pests away from your other plants.

Growing Garden Combinations

Growing companion plantings isn't very different from how you normally care for your garden. You still need to prepare the soil well, plant at the proper time, and water and fertilize as necessary. "Planting Companions," starting on page 64, and "Caring for Companions," starting on page 74, cover these basic techniques, with special tips on dealing with companions.

Sage, spinach, and borage are some of the companions that grow well with tomatoes.

If you just want to try out different combinations and aren't set on proving that they really work, you may try new companion plant groupings throughout your garden each year. If you really want to see how a certain grouping performs, though, you may want to set up more formal trials. Select two or more sites in the garden that have similar soil and exposure. Plant your crop with its companion in one spot and the crop alone in another spot as a control. If you have lots of room, repeat the plantings in several different areas.

Evaluating Companions

Throughout the season, observe the performance of the companion plantings you are testing. If you've set up a more formal experiment, compare the combination in question with the control plantings. Keep a notebook where you can record the setup and results of the trials. It's often difficult to definitely say that one system "worked" better than another. It helps if you concentrate on specific benefits, like yield or pest damage. (Did the interplanted crop produce more or less than the control planting? Which had more insect damage—the companion-planted crop or the control?)

To get the most out of companion planting, it's often wise to try a combination at least twice; three times is even better. Then you can look at the combination's overall performance and make an informed decision on whether it's worth trying again. You'll soon build a list of plants and techniques that will make your garden more productive and easier to maintain.

Mixing a variety of flower types can attract more beneficials.

Plant Antagonists

Just as some plants grow especially well together, a few are able to keep other kinds of plants from crowding in around them. This phenomenon is called allelopathy. Allelopathic plants work by releasing inhibitory chemicals into the soil or air—a neat trick for making sure nothing is going to compete with a plant for its share of rooting space, moisture, and nutrients.

Chemical compounds released by some living plants and many decomposing plants—including legumes, grains, brassicas, and marigolds—can lower yields of existing crop plants, kill seedlings, and limit seed germination. Garden mums (*Chrysanthemum* x *morifolium*), for instance, produce an allelopathic compound in their leaves. When the compound washes out of the leaves and falls to the ground, it prevents lettuce seeds from germinating. Red clover (*Trifolium pratense*) releases nine different compounds that prevent new red clover seedlings from sprouting. Gray sage (*Salvia leucophylla*) releases a volatile compound that drifts to earth nearby and stops the seedling growth of many species.

Researchers and gardeners are continually learning more about the ways different plants can squelch the growth of others. Here are more examples of allelopathic plants and their possible effects:

- Bear's-breech (*Acanthus mollis*) releases an allelopathic compound that can stunt the growth of cucumbers, oats, radishes, and cabbage. This compound also inhibits the growth of *Fusarium* and *Helminthosporium* fungi and discourages insect feeding.
- Broccoli and cabbage are widely allelopathic.
- Cereal crop residues tend to be allelopathic and inhibit some fungal growth. Barley and oats can inhibit nutrient absorption in pea and hairy vetch (although the legumes *encourage* it in barley and oats). Rye seedlings are strongly allelopathic but grow more benign as they mature.
- Common wormwood (*Artemisia absinthium*) can interfere with plant growth, especially when interplanted with other herbs.
- Corn, when young, releases water-soluble compounds that are allelopathic and fungicidal.
- Eryngo (*Eryngium paniculatum*) seeds inhibit the

Some gardeners claim that potatoes can interfere with photosynthesis and nitrogen absorption in apple trees.

germination of velvetleaf (*Abutilon theophrasti*), a common field weed.
- Fennel can inhibit the growth of vegetables and herbs.
- Marigolds can be widely allelopathic while growing and decomposing.
- Common milkweed (*Asclepias syriaca*) can inhibit the growth of sorghum seedlings.
- Papaya seeds can inhibit germination in other seeds.
- Peppergrass (*Lepidium* spp.), evening primroses (*Oenothera* spp.), and crabgrass (*Digitaria* spp.) can stop germination of other seeds, including crown vetch (*Coronilla varia*).

Fennel and potatoes may inhibit the growth of tomatoes, while black walnuts can cause tomatoes to wilt and die.

Beware of Black Walnuts

Of all the plants with allelopathic properties, black walnut (*Juglans nigra*) is probably the most notorious. It was noted as far back as 50 A.D. that many plants grew poorly near this tree. We now know that black walnuts contain a compound called juglone. (Juglone is the material that will dye your hands brown if you handle ripe walnut husks.)

Rain dissolves juglone from the leaves and washes it down into the rooting area, killing or stunting many kinds of plants. Rhododendrons, blackberries, tomatoes, alfalfa, and apple trees are often affected. A few plants that usually tolerate juglone include onions, corn, raspberries, grapes, forsythia, and Kentucky bluegrass. Which plants survive under walnuts and which ones don't can vary widely from place to place, depending on factors like the soil conditions and the amount of rainfall. If you have black walnut trees, it's usually a trial-and-error process to see what plants will thrive or merely survive in your particular garden conditions.

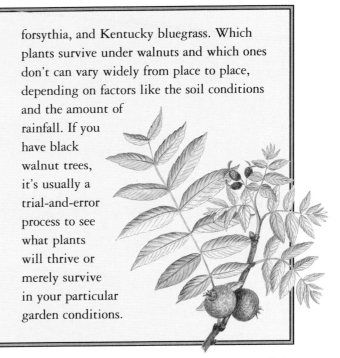

- Sunflower (*Helianthus annuus*) is widely allelopathic and also inhibits nitrogen fixation. The seed hulls contain a compound similar to juglone, the allelopathic material released by black walnuts.

Dealing with Difficult Plants

What does allelopathy mean for your garden? Whenever possible, keep strongly allelopathic plants like black walnuts and piles of sunflower hulls away from planting areas to reduce the chance of crop damage.

Quack grass, a common perennial weed, may make soil nutrients less available to your corn crop.

(Woven landscape fabrics or paving stones around the base of bird feeders make it easier to clean up seed hulls and avoid the patches of bare lawn under the feeder.)

In many cases, it's hard to identify when allelopathy is at work. The actual effect can be influenced by the soil, the amount of rainfall, and the plants themselves. If some of your crops are growing poorly and you've ruled out diseases and nutrient imbalances, consider that allelopathy might be the cause and try growing those plants elsewhere next year.

Allelopathy isn't always a problem in the garden. You may want to try using allelopathy to your advantage for keeping weeds and other vegetation under control. Annual rye (*Secale cereale*) is particularly useful for this in the vegetable garden. As it decomposes, it suppresses the growth of weeds such as redroot pigweed (*Amaranthus retroflexus*), common ragweed (*Ambrosia artemisiifolia*), and green foxtail (*Setaria viridis*). Grow it as a cover crop, and turn it under while potent and young to clean out weedy soil. (Let green manures and other crop residues that you work into the soil decompose completely before replanting.) Or grow a separate plot of rye in the garden, and clip the growth regularly to use as mulch.

Paving stones catch allelopathic sunflower hulls and prevent lawn damage.

COMPANION PLANTING

FOR PEST CONTROL

Of all the benefits you can get from companion planting, pest control is probably the most enticing. After all, wouldn't it be great if all your garden plants could protect each other, without any help from you? Well, companion planting won't get rid of all your problems, but it can help reduce the damage caused by many garden pests.

Effective companion planting begins with your observations, a bit of research, and some planning. Start by identifying the problems you currently have in the garden. Which plants are not growing well? Are they bothered by pests or some disease or deficiency? Are there holes in the leaves? You could be dealing with chewing pests like beetles, slugs, snails, or caterpillars. Finding tunnels in stems? Chances are good it's borer attack. Do any plants have distorted growth? If so, it's probably evidence of sucking insects like aphids, thrips, and leafhoppers. Inspect under the leaves and along the stems carefully; some plant-eaters hide there. Other pests come out at night and can be difficult to find. Look for them in the dark with a flashlight, or search for their hiding places under mulch or rocks during the daytime.

If you can't find out what problem is affecting your plant, or if you find an insect that you can't identify, take a sample of the pest or damaged plant to a nearby botanical garden or your local Cooperative Extension Service office for identification.

Once you know which pest you're dealing with, it's time to do some research. Look in gardening books or insect field guides to learn all you can about the pest. Find out when the pest appears and whether it attacks just certain crops or a wide range of different plants.

Armed with this information, you're ready to select the most appropriate plant combinations. Companion plants that work by repelling are most effective against pests like cabbage loopers that feed on only one or a few related crops. Pests that attack many different crops—like Japanese beetles—may simply move away from the repellent plants and feed in another area of the garden. For pests with wide-ranging appetites, you'll need to combine several strategies, such as encouraging natural predators with nursery crops and spreading trap plants throughout the garden.

This chapter details these and many other pest-fighting techniques you can use when companion planting. In "How Plants Control Pests" on page 24 you'll learn about the defenses plants have developed to protect themselves from attack. "Companions as Repellents" on page 26 tells how plants can fend off pests and prevent crop damage. "Companions as Nursery Crops" on page 28 discusses how they can attract the beneficial insects that prey upon plant-eating insects. In "Weeds and Your Crops" on page 30 you'll learn about the beneficial and harmful ways weeds can interact with your garden plants. And "Decoy and Trap Crops" on page 32 explains how plants that actually attract pests like aphids and flea beetles can be useful in controlling garden problems.

Sunflowers are popular garden plants for their large, colorful flowers and tasty seeds. They can also help to attract beneficial insects like hover flies and honeybees to control pests and pollinate other crops.

Growing flowers with vegetables adds some diversity, but pests can still find crops easily in mass plantings.

Mixed gardens of flowers, fruits, vegetables, and herbs make it difficult for pests to track down their food.

How Plants Control Pests

Plants have a number of strategies they can use to discourage pests. Some plants rely on one method; others use a combination of pest-fighting properties.

Making Detection Difficult

Just as you may be drawn to the aroma of grilled steak or freshly cooked pizza, some pests rely on their sense of smell to find an appropriate food source. The cucumber beetle, for instance, is attracted to cucumber plants by the presence of cucurbitacin, a bitter-flavored compound. Fewer beetles are attracted to cucurbitacin-free cultivars. (Unfortunately, cucurbitacin-free cucumber cultivars are *more* appealing to spider mites!)

Other pests key in on their targets using color. Whiteflies, aphids, cucumber beetles, fungus gnats, onion flies, carrot rust flies, cabbage root flies, and imported cabbageworms are attracted to yellowish colors. As a result, you can fool pests by planting off-color versions of their favorite crop. For example, red cabbage, purple cauliflower, and purple kohlrabi are less attractive to cabbage loopers and imported cabbageworms. Yellow berries attract fewer birds than red berries. Japanese beetles are less tempted to feed on dark-colored flowers.

Some plants are less attractive to pests because of their physical structure or location. Aphids prefer to feed in the shade, so they'll bypass more exposed lanky pea vines in favor of densely branched plants. Flea beetles prefer the sun, so they are less common on crops that receive some shade.

Repelling the Attack

Once pests find a target, they must break through the plant's first line of defense—its epidermis, or skin. Some plants have tough, hairy, or waxy leaves that make penetration difficult. Hairy-leaved cherry tomatoes, for instance, resist many chewing insects.

Other kinds of physical adaptations can help to reduce pest damage. Corn ears with long, tight husks are less prone to damage by birds or corn earworms. Beans and peas with tough, leathery pods are less susceptible to weevil injury.

The unusual colors of red cabbage, purple cauliflower, and purple kohlrabi may confuse pests and minimize damage.

Tomatoes attacked by pests release compounds that can alert nearby crops to produce materials toxic to insects.

Fighting Back

Once attacked, plants aren't always passive victims—many have developed ways to fight back. When damaged, most plants produce a variety of repellent compounds called phytoalexins. Phytoalexins can be stored in little packages within plant cells. When the cell is broken by a nibbling pest, the repellent is released, encouraging the pest to feed elsewhere.

Sometimes the defenses of one plant can protect another kind of plant from pests. University of Delaware research showed that extracts from tansy plants sprayed on eggplant foliage kept Colorado potato

Hairy foliage may deter some pests, but not all attackers are so easily discouraged. Japanese beetles will still feed on borage, hairy leaves and all.

beetle larvae from feeding for more than 22 hours. A Washington State University Institute of Biological Science study showed that pest-attacked tomatoes can warn other plants to produce more phytoalexins. In this study, tomatoes attacked by pests released a perfumy fragrance (methyl jasmonate) that caused nearby tomato, tobacco, and alfalfa plants to manufacture compounds poisonous to insects.

Some plants have a less-aggressive strategy. Instead of fighting back, they simply tolerate pests or diseases. Tolerant plants grow quickly enough to remain healthy and reach reproductive size before pests cause too much damage. With good care and regular watering and fertilizing, you can encourage almost all plants to make strong, healthy growth that is naturally less susceptible to pests and diseases.

If birds are a problem, try yellow- or orange-fruited plants; they are often less attractive to birds than red fruit.

Spraying cabbage with a solution of southernwood and water may help repel imported cabbageworms.

Physical barriers like hedges and fences can help intercept flying pests as they travel into your yard.

Some companion gardeners claim that castor bean plants will repel moles, voles, and other animal pests.

Companions as Repellents

Take advantage of the natural ways plants can control pests in your own garden. You can mask the scent of crops with more pungent species, use plants or their extracts to disturb or kill pests, or create physical barriers to keep flying insects away from your crops. If you're feeling adventurous, you may even decide to experiment with plants that are said to repel animal pests.

Creating "Chemical" Barriers

Powerfully scented plants produce various chemical compounds that tend to discourage most pests. Bold lemony or perfumy fragrances, given off by volatile essential oils in mints, thyme, lemon balm, and lemon geranium, often make pests flee. Many herbs produce these aromatic compounds, making them natural choices for companion plants. Mixing these pungent plants among pest-prone crops may help mask the scent of the crops and keep insects guessing.

Garlic is another strongly scented plant with a long reputation as a companion plant. It is often recommended for interplanting with roses or tomatoes to repel pests. Garlic

Fragrant herbs like lemon balm, scented geraniums, and thyme are popular repellents.

does contain compounds that will kill pests like aphids, onion flies, and mosquitoes, as well as beneficial insects such as lacewings and lady beetles. It also has fungicidal and bactericidal properties and has been known to protect tomatoes and potatoes from blights. Garlic extracts are even more powerful. For more information on using garlic extracts for pest control, see "Dealing with Pests and Diseases" on page 84.

Building Physical Barriers

Companion plants also can intercept pests physically. Flying insects often ride the breezes, alighting wherever they find a suitable plant to make into a meal. If you can interrupt their flight path with an inedible item, you may be able to limit their access to your crop plants. Block the prevailing wind with a fence, trellis, hedge, screen, or alley planting (see "Alley Cropping" on page 38, for details on this particular technique). Surround your garden with herbaceous plants such as sunflowers that are tall in summer when your pest problems are at their peak.

Use deciduous

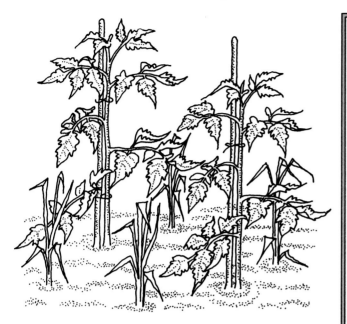

Garlic and onions interplanted with tomatoes may help repel pests with their powerful odors.

bushes to screen your garden throughout the growing season; plant evergreen shrubs and trees to block the wind year-round. Leafy barriers such as these serve a double purpose as shelter for beneficial insects.

Controlling Animals with Plants

People are the only animals that enjoy spicy or strongly aromatic foods. You can make use of this fact to discourage other kinds of creatures from browsing in your gardens. Try surrounding your garden with boldly scented or spicy herbs and vegetables for an edging that you will enjoy but animals won't.

Certain plants have been labeled especially good for repelling deer, rabbits, moles, and similar nuisances. According to folklore, seeds of castor beans (*Ricinus communis*) planted 5 or 6 feet (1.5 or 1.8 m) apart around the garden will keep out moles and deer. (Use caution if you have kids, though—this plant is toxic enough to kill a child who eats several of the seeds.) The mole plant (*Euphorbia lathyrus*) is said to be a deterrent for mice, gophers, and moles. This plant, like most of the spurge family (Euphorbiaceae), has white sap that is bitter and irritating. Some gardeners claim that you can annoy gophers by planting it next to their holes or by spacing plants every 5 feet (1.5 m) around the garden as a barrier.

In both cases, unfortunately, there is nothing stopping pests from simply going around any unpleasant barrier you plant. A more surefire way to control animal pests is to surround your garden with a fence. Make it up to 8 feet (2.4 m) high for deer or 2 feet (60 cm) high and 6 inches (15 cm) deep for rabbits.

Marigolds for Nematodes

Marigolds are probably the most widely grown companion plants. Many gardeners swear by their power to repel all kinds of pests.

So far, scientists have only been able to show that marigolds can affect root knot nematodes and root lesion nematodes, microscopic soil-dwelling pests. The roots and, to a lesser extent, the shoots produce compounds called thiophenes. Researchers are not sure whether these chemical compounds kill nematodes outright or if the nematodes become trapped within marigold roots and the thiophenes keep them from reproducing.

No matter how they work, you can use marigolds to clear nematodes out of the soil before or after planting susceptible crops. Plant any cultivar of French or American marigolds, or try the extrapotent, 7-foot (2.1 m) tall 'Nemakill'. For best results, space the plants evenly over the bed. Chop up the tall stems, and turn everything under at the end of the season. As marigolds decay, they'll kill anything you plant. But by spring, the soil is safe for planting again.

In Dutch studies, marigolds have also suppressed nematodes when interplanted in containers with nematode-susceptible crops. Unfortunately, attempts to extract the nematocidal compound from the marigold foliage and pour it on infested soils have not been successful.

In most cases, you're safer relying on sturdy fences than on plants to keep animal pests out of your plantings.

Fennel, dill, buckwheat, cosmos, and tansy are a few nursery crops that attract and shelter lady beetles.

Companions as Nursery Crops

Nursery crops—plants that provide food and shelter for pest-eating insects—serve a valuable function in any kind of garden. They encourage the beneficials to make a home in your yard, supplement their diets when pests are in short supply, and offer nourishment to the nonpredatory stages of these insects. (Adult lacewings, for example, feed mostly on nectar, though their larvae are voracious aphid predators.)

How Nursery Crops Help

Almost all plants can shelter beneficials, but some plants have characteristics that make them particularly enticing. Most beneficial insects prefer flowers that are small and abundant, like the tightly packed flower heads of yarrow or coneflowers or the bloom clusters of thyme and catnip. These flowers provide easily accessible sources of nectar and pollen that many beneficials need to supplement their diet when pests are scarce.

To attract and keep the widest variety of beneficials, make sure something suitable is in bloom throughout the growing season for a constant supply of food. Mix the attractant plants amid the plants you want to protect, so the predators and

Dill, Queen-Anne's-lace, and their relatives produce nectar-rich flowers.

A "bug bath"—basically a shallow pan with stones and water—will help attract more beneficials to your yard.

parasites will always be close to your crops and ready to go to work when pests appear. Watch for egg cases on pest bodies—a sign that the system is working.

Best Plants for Beneficials

Over the years, researchers and gardeners have identified many specific plants that beneficials find particularly enticing. Some of the best are mentioned below—grouped by their botanical family—along with an explanation of their attractant characteristics.

Daisy Family (Compositae) What we call a daisy flower is actually a large collection of very small, specialized flowers. These blooms are excellent sources of both pollen and nectar and attract a wide variety of beneficial insects, including parasitic wasps, hover flies,

Catnip (*Nepeta cataria*) and other plants that produce small individual flowers can attract many beneficials.

Lavender, bee balm, and other mint-family members can draw beneficial insects to protect your garden plantings.

green lacewings, assassin bugs, and lady beetles.

Among the annual composites, try cosmos, calliopsis (*Coreopsis tinctoria*), marigolds, sunflowers, China asters (*Callistephus chinensis*), and dahlias. Perennials include coreopsis (*Coreopsis* spp.), tansy (*Tanacetum vulgare*), golden marguerite (*Anthemis tinctoria*), perennial sunflowers (*Helianthus* spp.), goldenrods (*Solidago* spp.), coneflowers (*Rudbeckia* and *Echinacea* spp.), asters, and gayfeathers (*Liatris* spp.).

Mint Family (Labiatae) Plants in this family tend to have aromatic foliage and clusters of many small, two-lipped flowers. The flowers can attract bees, hover flies, and other beneficial insects.

Among the annuals, try basil or sweet marjoram (*Origanum majorana*). Perennials include thyme, mint, garden sage (*Salvia officinalis*), lavender, hyssop (*Hyssopus officinalis*), wild marjoram (*Origanum vulgare*), catmints (*Nepeta* spp.), Russian sage (*Perovskia atriplicifolia*), and bee balms (*Monarda* spp.).

Carrot Family (Umbelliferae) The blooms of plants in this family bear small flowers grouped into large,

Adding flowering herbs and ornamentals to your vegetable garden helps keep pest-eating insects where you need them.

umbrella-shaped clusters. They can attract lady beetles, hover flies, parasitic wasps, spiders, lacewings, and other beneficial insects.

Favorite annuals include dill (*Anethum graveolens*), caraway (*Carum carvi*), and fennel (*Foeniculum vulgare*). Also try the biennial Queen-Anne's-lace (*Daucus carota* var. *carota*) and perennial angelicas (*Angelica* spp.).

Miscellaneous Flowers Other flowers that will attract beneficial insects include butterfly flower (*Asclepias tuberosa*), other milkweeds (*Asclepias* spp.), and alliums like chives (*Allium schoenoprasum*). You also can try green manures like buckwheat (*Fagopyrum esculentum*), sweet clovers (*Melilotus* spp.), and white clovers (*Trifolium* spp.). Beneficial insects also visit the flowers of weeds such as lamb's-quarters, dandelion, goldenrod, pigweed, knotweed, and wild mustard. (You probably wouldn't want to plant these, but you could leave a few of them unweeded if they pop up in an unused corner of the garden.)

Asters, cosmos, dahlias, and other daisy-flowered plants are excellent sources of pollen and nectar for beneficials.

Create the Right Environment

If you create the right environment, you can attract enough beneficial insects to keep pest problems to a minimum.

- Provide "bug baths"—shallow dishes of water filled with small rocks for perches.
- Include groundcovers, mulches, and stepping-stone paths in your garden plans; these undisturbed spots form excellent hiding places for rove and ground beetles.
- Plant a variety of plant species with different heights and shapes to provide shelter for a wide variety of predators.
- Install a fence or hedge as a windbreak to reduce dust; dusty conditions cause beneficials to dehydrate quickly.

Weeds and Your Crops

To many gardeners, weeds rank right up there with insects and diseases as garden problems. But just as not all insects are pests, not all weeds are bad. In fact, some of them have particular virtues that make them tolerable (if not welcome) in the companion garden. Dandelions, for instance, root deeply, breaking up compacted soil and bringing up nutrients. Goldenrods and oxeye daisy attract beneficial insects. Wild mustard and pigweed can trap insect pests, luring them away from your crops. Low-growing weeds, such as purslane and knotweed, can keep the soil cool and shaded. And corn cockle can release compounds that help other plants grow. If carefully managed, some weeds can make useful companions.

Managing Weeds as Companions

Before you allow any weeds to stay in your garden, you should get to know a bit about them. Find out if they have rampantly spreading roots that are difficult to curb or if you need to deadhead so the weed won't set a bucketful of seeds; otherwise, the weeds will move in and consume most of the space you had intended for your own plants. Some weeds can harbor the same diseases as your crops, making them poor companions; other weeds attract the same

Purplish pink corn cockle is a pretty wheat weed, but avoid its poisonous seed as you harvest the wheat.

pests, making the weeds excellent trap crops. Here is the lowdown on some of the most common garden weeds:

• Corn cockle (*Agrostemma githago*): This softly hairy, purple-flowered plant grows well with winter rye and wheat. Studies have shown that corn cockle produces agrostemmin, a compound that improves the growth of wheat. (Be aware, though, that the seed of corn cockle is poisonous and can be a danger if ground with wheat into flour.)

• Jimsonweed (*Datura stramonium*): This

Regular weeding keeps your garden looking good, but some kinds of weeds can actually benefit your crops.

Dandelions are normally considered a nuisance, but they can be helpful for loosening tough, compacted soil.

Removing weeds from around young plants will help crops get off to a good start; later weeding is less critical.

Oxeye daisies, goldenrod, and other flowering weeds can attract beneficial insects to your garden.

candidate for a trap crop.
- Mustards, wild (*Brassica* spp.): Annual mustards have toothed or lobed leaves and four-petaled yellow flowers. They can serve as a trap crop for cabbage pests.
- Nightshade, black (*Solanum nigrum*): This poisonous annual has slightly toothed leaves and tomato-like flowers. It may trap Colorado potato beetles and kill the larvae, but it also will carry pests and diseases that attack tomatoes, peppers, and eggplants.
- Pigweed, redroot (*Amaranthus retroflexus*): This prolifically seeding annual has red stems and a deep taproot that helps condition soils.
- Queen-Anne's-lace (*Daucus carota* var. *carota*): This biennial has feathery leaves and a lacy umbrella-shaped head of white flowers that attract beneficial insects. It also has a deep taproot that can break up compacted soil. If you leave plants in the garden, remove spent flowers to prevent reseeding.

poisonous annual has toothed leaves, stems as high as 5 feet (1.5 m), and trumpet-shaped flowers. It shares the same diseases and pests of peppers, potatoes, and other members of the tomato family. It may be a good trap crop for Colorado potato beetles.
- Lamb's-quarters (*Chenopodium album*): The silvery, triangular leaves and the shoots of this annual are very attractive to aphids, making it a good

Unwelcome Weeds

Although some weeds do have redeeming properties, many of the plants that spring up in your garden are aggressive and undesirable. Perennials such as bindweed, sorrel, and ground ivy spread by creeping roots or stems and take a lot of hand weeding to eliminate. Even "beneficial" weeds like lamb's-quarters and wild mustards can take over if you let them set seed. Large numbers of weeds can compete with your crops for light, water, and nutrients. Certain weeds—including crabgrass, peppergrass, curly dock, and common milkweed—are even allelopathic and can prevent other plants from growing nearby. (To learn more about allelopathy, see "Plant Antagonists" on page 20.

Weeds can also carry pests and diseases that

attack garden plants. Catnip, milkweed, and pokeweed can carry cucumber mosaic virus, a problem on most crops of the squash family. Wild cherries can be infested with black knot fungi that will attack cultivated cherry trees; wild apples and pears can be a reservoir for the infectious bacterial disease fire blight. Wild asters can carry a wilt disease. When diseases are a problem, don't take a chance— eliminate weedy disease sources, despite any virtues they may have.

If you have extra space in your garden, consider trying decoy or trap plants to lure pests from your crops.

Decoy and Trap Crops

Growing plants that you *know* pests will flock to? It may sound crazy, but it's just another way to use companion plants to your advantage. The trick is to cultivate a few plants that pests find more attractive than your good crops. The pests will be more likely to damage the decoy plants than your crops. And once the pests have congregated on the trap crop, you can easily destroy them.

Trap cropping does have a few drawbacks you should consider before depending on it for your entire pest-control strategy. Trap cropping takes some advance planning and careful, continued observation. It consumes productive space and will not produce a harvest—a potential problem in a small garden. And if you choose to bag and discard infested plants, you also may be destroying beneficial insects or their future generations. But with some care and an understanding of the commitment involved, trap cropping can be a worthwhile part of your overall pest control program.

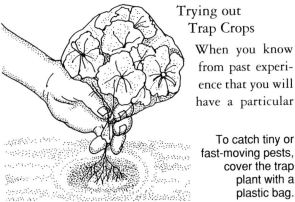

Trying out Trap Crops

When you know from past experience that you will have a particular

To catch tiny or fast-moving pests, cover the trap plant with a plastic bag.

kind of insect problem on your crops, follow the guidelines below to set a trap for that pest.

Get the Timing Right The trap crop must be growing when the pests are out in force. If the pest problem only occurs at one time of year—for example, cabbage maggots and carrot beetles can be worst in spring—a single planting of a trap crop may be enough to control them. But if the pest is in action all summer, you may need to plant a succession of crops. Use your garden notes from previous years, ask gardening neighbors, or look in pest-control books to find out when the pest in question is most active so you can time the trap crop planting accordingly.

Here's an example of how trap cropping can work to lure aphids away from roses. As soon as the last spring frost passes, plant clumps of nasturtium seedlings beside your rose bush. (Starting with plants instead of direct-sown seed is important since the nasturtiums need to take root before the first generation of aphids becomes a real problem.) As  soon as you find the aphids swarming on the nasturtiums, destroy the plants and pests promptly so the aphids don't reproduce. For continued trap cropping, sow nasturtium seed every 2 weeks until midsummer.

Keep Trap Crops Close Grow the trap plants as near as you can to the plants bothered by pests. Plant the traps beside ornamentals, in between rows in the vegetable garden, or intermingled in wide beds.

Watch Traps Carefully Once the trap is set, be ready to kill the pests before they breed or move on.

Lantana and tomatoes are two favorite food sources for whiteflies. Try planting a few extras as trap crops.

Nearby plantings of borage, dill, and lovage can lure pesky hornworms away from your tomato plants.

A companion crop of nasturtiums can help protect your roses from aphids. Destroy the trap crop when it is infested.

Female aphids, for instance, give birth to live baby aphids, which mature to reproductive age within 2 weeks. If you let an aphid trap crop go unobserved for 2 weeks, you could multiply the aphid problem instead of solving it.

Choose a Control When you find that your trap crop is infested, you have several ways to go about eliminating the pests. You can do away with most of the pests, leaving a few for beneficial insects to dine upon; pick off and destroy large, slow pests like tomato hornworms or cabbage loopers (unless they are covered with white cocoons, which indicate that the pests have been parasitized by beneficials); or shake crawling pests like beetles and weevils off of trap plants in the cool morning or evening, when pests are moving more slowly, and catch them on the ground in a towel or sheet of newspaper. Pick or dump pests into a bucket of soapy water.

To trap tiny or fast-moving pests, cover the entire plant gently with a plastic bag. (You may want to pick off and release any beneficials you see on the plant before bagging it.) Use a twist tie to seal the bag opening around the plant stem. Then uproot and discard the bag, bugs and all.

Try These as Trap Crops

Some pests have a particular plant that draws them like a magnet. They will shun less-favored plants to nibble upon their favorites. Here's a list of some common garden pests and the crops they find especially enticing:

- Colorado potato beetles are attracted to black nightshade.
- Cabbageworms and harlequin bugs will swarm away from cabbage plants to mustard plants.
- Flea beetles and aphids are drawn to nasturtiums.
- Cabbage maggots will riddle radishes rather than broccoli, cauliflower, and cabbage.

Shake slow-moving pests like beetles and weevils onto a sheet of paper. Dump pests into a bucket of soapy water.

INTERPLANTING

Interplanting—the time-tested system of growing two or more crops in the same place, at the same time—is one of the most exciting techniques you can try in the vegetable garden. Interplanting helps you make the most efficient use of available space, possibly doubling or even tripling your current yields without increasing your labor or the size of your garden.

In many ways, interplanting and companion planting are very similar. Many gardeners, in fact, use the words interchangeably. But to be accurate, interplanting relies on choosing plants with the most compatible growth habits and needs so you can fit the most plants in the smallest amount of space. Companion planting also combines compatible crops, but it concentrates on grouping plants with specific properties—like repellent odors or nitrogen production—so plants can directly benefit each other.

In this chapter, you'll learn all the basics of successful interplanting techniques. Even if you never get far into companion planting, following these proven methods will help to increase your garden yields greatly.

If you *do* plan on extensive companion plantings, considering these techniques will help you create even more effective combinations.

In the pages that follow, you'll learn the secrets to grouping plants that grow well together. "Create Effective Combinations" on page 36 provides an overview of planning productive garden groupings. "Alley Cropping" on page 38 is a special technique of combining nitrogen-producing trees and shrubs with your vegetable crops. "Consider Life Cycles" on page 40 explains how the varying growth speeds of different crops can influence their value as companions. "Organize Crops by Growth Habits" on page 42 tells how height and spread can influence crop compatibility above ground, while "Plan around Rooting Patterns" on page 44 explains how the belowground parts interact. "Combine Compatible Nutrient Needs" on page 46 and "Think about Light and Shade Tolerance" on page 48 cover the feeding habits and light requirements that you need to consider when planning an interplanting system for your vegetable garden.

The key to interplanting is combining plants that have compatible needs and growing habits. In ornamental gardens, you can create beautiful groupings; in the vegetable garden, you'll get higher yields and healthier plants.

Create Effective Combinations

The trick to effective interplanting is grouping plants that will make the best use of the space that you have. In cities, planners make efficient use of the available space by building up into the sky and down into the earth. A well-planned garden can be organized the same way, with each plant occupying its own particular place above and below the ground.

In the flower garden, you probably base planting choices around factors like color or bloom time. In the vegetable garden, you'll have other criteria for interplanting. You may want to grow more produce in a limited space or spread out your harvest so only a few fresh vegetables are ripening at any given time. Once you decide *why* you want to interplant, you can choose what to grow and determine how those plants will fit together in the garden.

Consider These Characteristics

Several factors can determine why one grouping is a success and another is a dismal failure. Understanding these factors will help you plan the best possible combinations for your crops.

Life Cycles The term "life cycle" refers to the various stages (including birth, growth, reproduction, and death) an organism goes through during its existence. In the garden, we're often concerned with how long it takes our plants to go through these stages. Annuals—including corn, beans, and radishes—complete their life cycles in 1 year, while biennials

Radishes grow fast and take up little room, making them good companions for slower plants.

(such as parsley) take 2 years and perennials (like asparagus and sage) live for several to many years.

In the vegetable garden, it's generally easiest to plant crops with similar life cycles together. Mixing annuals and perennials can be tricky, since you will disturb the roots of the perennials each year when you prepare the soil for planting the annuals. If you want them for their leaves, biennials are usually grown with and treated like annuals. But if you want the flowers or seeds, the plants must stay in place for 2 years and should then be treated more like perennials. "Consider Life Cycles" on page 40 explains in more detail how to use plant life cycles to your advantage when planning interplantings.

Growth Habits The height and spread of plants also affects whether or not they make good companions. At close spacings, two spreading plants (such as melons and sweet potatoes) will tend to crowd each other as they compete for room. But combining a spreading plant with an upright plant—like corn with squash—allows room for both to develop properly. Tall plants can shade shorter plants, which can be an advantage for shade-tolerant crops like lettuce but harmful for sun-lovers like beans and onions. "Organize Crops by Growth

Orange coneflowers (*Rudbeckia* spp.) and summer squash make an attractive and productive combination.

The different growth habits and nutrient needs of lettuce and onions make them ideal garden companions.

Bushy, low-growing crops like squash share space well with tall, upright plants like corn and sunflowers.

Experiment with Interplanting

Once you've identified your goal for interplanting, you can develop a solution based on your knowledge of the plants and their characteristics. Here are some examples of how the planning process works.

Your goal: To keep weeds down and enrich the soil in your pumpkin patch.

The solution: Plant pumpkin hills between rows of nitrogen-fixing clover. The mature clover plants can provide extra nitrogen for the pumpkins.

Your goal: To get more of a harvest out of your corn planting.

The solution: Plant pole beans between the corn rows. Give the corn several weeks' head start, or plant the beans near old stalks that have finished producing ears.

Your goal: To plant a crop that can fill the space around the asparagus bed before the asparagus foliage fills out.

The solution: Plant parsley, which thrives in spring sun and tolerates light summer shade. The asparagus roots will run deeper than the parsley, so they won't compete for moisture. But both are heavy feeders, so add extra compost or fertilizer each year.

Habits" on page 42 offers more details on combining plants with compatible sizes.

Rooting Patterns Just as plants grow to different heights and spreads above ground, their roots have different structures and grow in different soil zones below ground. For best results, match shallow-rooted plants with those that have deep roots, and combine finely branched fibrous root systems with thick taproots. Spinach, for instance, has shallow fibrous roots, which makes it a good companion for deeper-rooted crops like tomatoes and beans. "Plan around Rooting Patterns" on page 44 covers the root structures of common garden plants in greater detail.

Nutrient Needs Make the most efficient use of available soil nutrients by combining plants that have complementary needs. Onions, for instance, are light feeders, while lettuce—a heavy feeder—draws a higher amount of nutrients from the soil. If you group plants with similar needs, they will compete for nutrients, and both crops may suffer. "Combine Compatible Nutrient Needs" on page 46 discusses the particular needs of many common crops.

Light and Shade Tolerance Above ground, the tops of plants compete for the available light. Many plants thrive in full sunlight, which you can provide by spacing plants far enough apart that they don't shade one another. But if space is limited, you can combine plants with compatible light needs at close spacings and still get good yields. Beets, for instance, can tolerate a bit of shade, so they make excellent companions for sun-loving bush beans. "Think about Light and Shade Tolerance" on page 48 explains the needs of popular garden plants in more detail.

Tall crops planted to the south or west of shorter crops will provide shade for them.

Like other members of the pea family, black locust (*Robinia pseudoacacia*) trees can add nitrogen to the soil.

Alley Cropping

Who has ever heard of planting trees and shrubs in the vegetable garden? Aren't you supposed to keep your vegetable crops *away* from tall, shade-casting plants? Yes, normally trees and shrubs are kept separate from vegetables, but it doesn't *have* to be that way. Some woody plants can actually benefit vegetable crops by adding nitrogen to the soil. And harvesting the succulent stems of fast-growing woody plants can provide lots of organic material for mulching, while preventing the plants from getting tall enough to shade your

Shrubby moss locust (*Robinia hispida*) can be an attractive and productive choice for alley cropping.

crops. If you have some extra space and like to try new methods, you may want to experiment with the technique known as alley cropping.

How Alley Cropping Works

Alley cropping layouts use narrow rows of trees or shrubs between 5- to 20-foot (1.5 to 6 m) strips of crop planting area. Cutting the trees back regularly promotes the production of soft, leafy stems, which in turn can be harvested and used as a nitrogen-rich mulch for the

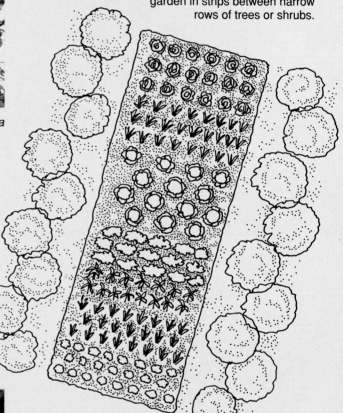

Start your own alley cropping system by planting your garden in strips between narrow rows of trees or shrubs.

vegetables. In between harvests, the trees help improve the site by preventing erosion, blocking strong winds, sheltering beneficial insects, and casting light shade to protect sun-sensitive crops.

Which Woody Plants Work Best?

Rhonda Janke, director of research at the Rodale Institute in Maxatawny, Pennsylvania, is trying out many different tree and shrub species to determine which work best for temperate-climate areas. She evaluates plants for their hardiness (to Zone 6), their ability to resprout after being harvested, and their ability to fix nitrogen (convert nitrogen gas in the air to a form that plants can use).

So far, Janke reports the best success with mimosa, black alder (*Alnus glutinosa*), false indigo (*Amorpha fruticosa*), bladder senna (*Colutea arborescens*), Russian olive (*Elaeagnus angustifolia*), moss locust (*Robinia hispida*), and black locust (*Robinia pseudoacacia*). Of these she suggests bladder senna, which has handsome yellow flowers, and false indigo, which has purple flowers, as the best choices for home gardeners. Since both have attractive blooms, they can double as ornamentals and garden crops.

Overall, though, the most productive species is the black locust. It can fix relatively high quantities of nitrogen, and it resprouts readily after cutting. It is most prolific if cut back in fall to about 20 inches (50 cm) high. The only difficulty with this species is that some of the trees can resprout many feet or yards away from the original trunk. This weedy tendency could interfere with crop growth between the tree rows and could be a problem in smaller home gardens.

How to Make Your Own Alley Planting

Experimenting with alley cropping can be easy and fun. Simply follow the steps below.

1. Pick a site. You may decide to try alley cropping within your existing vegetable garden or as a border around the growing area. If you have extra space, you may want to set up the alley cropping area in a different

Once you cut back the woody stems, you can chip them for use as mulch around your vegetables and ornamentals.

spot so you can compare the results with your regular garden. Either way, the site for your planting should have all the characteristics of a regular vegetable garden—plenty of sunlight, good drainage, and well-prepared soil.

2. Pick a plant. Choose a nitrogen-fixing tree or shrub; try a black locust or experiment with a different species mentioned previously.

3. Plant the rows. Plant young trees or shrubs about 2 feet (60 cm) apart in rows 5 feet (1.5 m) wide, with 5 to 20 feet (1.5 to 6 m) of garden space in between. Prepare the soil between the tree rows as usual, and plant your crops each season.

4. Harvest the rows. Once the woody plants are established (after a year or two), cut them back near ground level and use the leaves and twigs as a mulch or an organic soil amendment. Use the larger branches to make trellises, flower stakes, or bean poles. In 1 or 2 years, when the woody plants resprout and reach a useful size, cut them again. If they begin to lose vigor after you've repeated the process several times, dig out the stumps and replant the rows with new trees.

If you have plenty of room, you may want to try black alder (*Alnus glutinosa*) in your alley plantings.

Bladder senna produces pretty yellow blooms and lots of useful growth.

Plantings that include perennials and trees call for careful planning, since they'll be in place for several years.

Consider Life Cycles

Part of creating productive interplantings is combining plants that have compatible life cycles. You may want to plant a fast grower—like radishes or lettuce—early in the season and follow it with a slower grower like tomatoes. Or you may want to interplant a fast grower like cabbage with a slow grower like onions: The fast crop will be ready for harvest by the time the slow-growing crop needs the space. Knowing a bit about the growth rates of your crops will help you choose plants that make good garden partners.

To get a better idea of the time plants will take to mature, start by learning a little about their lifetime strategies. Annuals, such as beans and basil, flower and produce fruits or seed within a single growing season. They die after setting seed or with the first killing fall frost. Biennials, like parsley and beets, produce roots and leaves one year and flowers the next year. They usually die after setting seed. Perennials, like rhubarb, asparagus, and thyme, can live for several years or several decades. Each type of plant has particular advantages for different planting schemes.

Quick-cropping Annuals

Fast-growing annuals such as leaf lettuce, cilantro (coriander), dill, kohlrabi, spinach, arugula, and radishes grow from seed to harvest quickly—often in just a few weeks. They make good companions for slower-growing crops, such as melons and brussels sprouts, since the fast growers will be harvested before the slow growers need the space. Fast growers can also flower quickly, so they are quick to attract beneficial insects. Quick-maturing annuals like mustard also make excellent trap crops; when the crop is covered with pests, destroy it and the pests, and replant. (For more information, see "Decoy and Trap Crops" on page 32.)

Moderately Fast Annuals

These annuals usually produce a crop within the span of a single 90-day season (i.e. spring, summer, fall, or,

Even if they don't bloom the first year, perennials with fragrant leaves (like lavender) can deter pests right away.

Annual flowers like cosmos will grow quickly and can attract beneficials to your garden from summer until frost.

in warm climates, winter). Since these moderately fast growers don't take up room the whole year, you can precede or follow them with a short-season crop like radishes or spinach. Some examples of moderately fast growers include beets, broccoli, bush lima beans, bush snap beans, cabbages, corn, cucumbers, eggplants, peas, okra, peppers, and tomatoes.

Long-season Annuals

Slow-growing crops like brussels sprouts, pole lima beans, melons, bulb onions, and pumpkins need most, if not all, of the growing season to mature. Plants in this group that have special pest-repelling qualities, such as onions, can be extra useful in a companion planting since they are effective for much of the growing season.

Biennials

The fact that biennials wait to flower until their second year is good news and bad news. The good news is that biennials—like parsley, beets, chicories, and carrots—seldom bolt (go to seed) during the first year of growth, so you're likely to get a good-quality harvest. But if you are growing biennials for their flowers (to attract beneficials) or their seeds, you have to wait 2 years.

With careful planning, you can use these characteristics to your advantage. Grow root-crop biennials like beets and carrots as annuals, and harvest the crop at the end of the season. Or mix leafy biennials like

Fast-growing chard is ready to pick as soon as 60 days from sowing, and it will keep producing all season.

parsley, caraway, and chicory into perennial plantings, harvesting the foliage the first season and enjoying the flowers or seeds the second year.

Perennials

Perennials can have a long and productive life in your garden, but they also are slower to reach maturity than annuals or biennials. If you are counting on them to attract beneficial insects with their flowers, you may have to wait 1 or 2 years before perennial seedlings bloom. You can cut the waiting time if you plant a large nursery plant or transplant a large division. Perennials with aromatic foliage, which include thyme, lavender, and yarrow, can be useful immediately after planting as pest deterrents.

Planning around Life Cycles

Take advantage of your crops' natural growth rates to create effective, high-yielding combinations. Here are a few ideas to get you started:

- Fill a garden bed all season with a succession of fast-growing annuals. Try a series like radishes, dill, and cilantro or arugula, leaf lettuce, and mustard.
- Interplant a fast grower with a moderately slow grower to get two harvests from the same space. The fast grower will be ready to pick before the slower crop needs the room. Try planting slow-growing brussels sprouts with speedy spinach or fast-growing carrots with slow-maturing onions.
- Pick compatible companions based on growth rates. For instance, if you want a plant that

will attract beneficials, that plant needs to be in flower during the vulnerable stages of its companion's life. Fast-growing calendulas, dill, cosmos, and buckwheat make great attractant companions for most annual crops. Once established, fall-blooming perennials like asters can attract beneficials to late plantings, such as broccoli or beets.

Organize Crops by Growth Habits

Think of your interplanted garden as a jigsaw puzzle. You need to piece together plants with complementary shapes so their foliage can spread over, under, or beside each other when they are planted closely. A carefully planned combination will take advantage of all the available growing space without crowding plants together, which would lead to stunted growth, poor performance, and possible disease problems.

Choosing Compatible Companions

Consider each crop's shape and size as you put together your garden puzzle. Tall, upright plants like corn, cosmos, Jerusalem artichokes, and sunflowers often form at least one edge of the planting. Site them on the south side of the garden to shade heat-sensitive crops like lettuce, or on the north side, where their shadow won't shade out sun-lovers like beans and peppers. Trellised plants, such as cucumbers, pole beans, or staked tomatoes, also need careful placement so they don't shade out shorter crops.

Some plants, like untrellised cucumbers, melons, oregano, pumpkins, sweet potatoes, and thyme, enjoy sprawling on the ground. These crops are good choices for covering the soil under tall upright crops such as corn. Just make sure that the tall crops are spaced far enough apart to avoid shading the sprawlers at their feet.

Most crops belong to an in-between category of

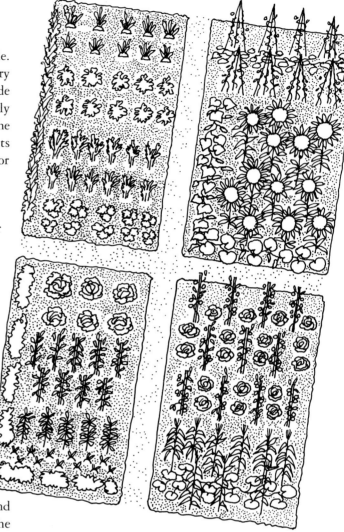

Without increasing the size of your garden, you can increase your harvests by combining plants with compatible growth habits. As you lay out the garden, consider growing tall or trellised plants with bushy or spreading, low-growing crops. The time you spend on careful planning will pay off during the growing season.

medium-sized plants. Some of these plants—like beets, carrots, and kohlrabi—tend to have a more narrow, upright habit; others—such as broccoli, cabbage, and bush beans—spread out more. Medium-sized upright and spreading plants tend to be compatible, as long as you give each crop enough space to develop without crowding.

Actual crop heights and shapes can vary widely, depending on cultural conditions and the cultivar you grow. Tomatoes, for instance, can either grow upward (if caged or trained) or sprawl (if unstaked or trellised). But the actual height

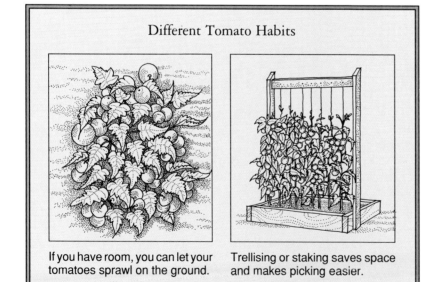

Different Tomato Habits

If you have room, you can let your tomatoes sprawl on the ground.

Trellising or staking saves space and makes picking easier.

Combining tall or upright plants with short or sprawling ones allows room for each to grow without crowding.

varies greatly depending on the cultivar; for example, the pot tomato 'Red Robin' stays 8 to 12 inches (20 to 30 cm) high, while 'Beefmaster' can reach 5 feet (1.5 m) high. Make sure you know the characteristics of the cultivars you choose so you can plan the siting and spacing accordingly. You also have to allow room at planting time for small seedlings to spread to their full size. Head lettuce, for example, starts as a seedling 3 inches (7.5 cm) high but can expand to 18 inches (45 cm) across. Plan ahead so interplantings will be compatible when they're both small and fully grown.

Some Super Groupings

Combining plants with complementary growth habits makes the most efficient use of garden space, since each plant can develop without crowding its neighbors. The possible combinations are almost endless, but here are a few suggestions to get you started:

Cool Season
- Broccoli (medium height, bushy) with beets (short, upright)
- Cabbage (short, bushy) with thyme (sprawling)
- Carrots (short, upright) with trellised peas (tall, upright)
- Spinach (short, bushy) with trellised peas (tall, upright)

Warm Season
- Bush beans (medium height, bushy) with summer savory (short, bushy)
- Corn (tall, upright) with squash (sprawling)
- Melons (sprawling) with sunflowers (tall, upright)
- Tomatoes (tall, bushy) with basil (short, bushy)
- Trellised cucumbers (tall, upright) with lettuce (short, bushy or upright)

Trellising is a great way to use garden space efficiently, and it makes harvesting a breeze. Plus, the trellises cast shade on their north and east sides, providing ideal conditions for summer spinach and lettuce.

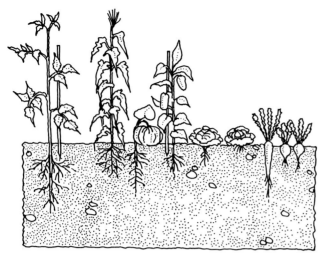

A combination of plants with different rooting depths will make the most effective use of soil nutrients.

Direct-sown tomatoes tend to form deep taproots; transplants have a shallower, branching root system.

Plan around Rooting Patterns

Just as your crops need to fit together well above ground, their root systems must be compatible, too. As you plan interplantings, combine crops that have different rooting depths so they can each form a vigorous, healthy root system without competing for space or resources.

Rooting Depths

Roots can form right at the soil surface or travel many feet below. Growing plants that occupy different rooting zones is an excellent way to make the most efficient use of soil resources like water and nutrients. It's especially important if you're combining two crops that have similar nutrient needs (such as shallower-rooted corn and deeper-rooted winter squash), so one crop can scavenge near the surface and the other can draw from nutrient reserves deeper in the soil.

Shallow-rooted Plants Shallow roots stay within two shovels' depths of the soil surface. Onions, celery, and other shallow-rooted crops need special attention, since their root systems are more exposed to the temperature and moisture changes near the soil surface. Be sure to mulch to minimize temperature changes in the root zone, and water shallow-rooted plants more frequently in dry weather. Since shallow roots don't dig far for nutrients, you may have to fertilize more frequently than you do for deep-rooted plants.

There are some tricks you can use to encourage shallow rooters like onions and celery to dig deeper and become more self-sufficient.

Alfalfa thrives on deep soil, where it can extend its taproot down in search of water and nutrients.

Deep-rooted pumpkins combine well with fibrous-rooted plants like corn or shallow rooters such as onions.

First, water deeply when you irrigate. If you use drip or trickle irrigation, provide water to all sides of the plant so the roots will not concentrate in the small, moist spots around the hoses or emitters. Also, keep the soil loose so roots can grow freely. Once you have prepared the soil in a garden bed, always walk *around* the bed—never *on* it—to avoid compaction. Build raised beds to provide more rooting area in shallow soil.

Deep-rooted Plants Deep-rooted plants, such as asparagus and parsnips, tend to be more drought-tolerant than shallow rooters. They can reach deep-down soil moisture, even during dry weather. They are better anchored and insulated from winter cold and summer heat. Some of these plants can break up deep layers of compacted soil and improve soil drainage. And because their roots travel down in the soil where other roots can't, they have more access to nutrients. Deep-rooted cover crops or green manures, like alfalfa and biennial sweet clovers (*Melilotus* spp.), are often used for this purpose. When the crops are worked into the soil, they enrich the upper soil layers as they decay.

Root Structures

The depth and width of any root system depends in part on the structure of the roots. Some plants have fibrous roots, which weave a fine-textured root network thickly through the soil. Celery, onions, and grasses usually have fibrous root systems. Other plants, including

Radishes are very shallow-rooted, making them good companions for a variety of deeper-rooting crops.

carrots and parsley, produce a thickened main taproot, which grows straight down. It sprouts roots along its length, but the youngest, most active roots are near the taproot tip. If the taproot is damaged—which happens if the plant is confined too long in a small pot, jostled during transplanting, or grown in shallow soil—it can revert into a fibrous root arrangement. Fibrous-rooted and taprooted plants tend to make good companions, since they tend to draw water and nutrients from different soil levels.

Rooting Depths of Common Crops

Interplanted combinations in a vegetable garden work better if the roots occupy different soil layers. Interplanting crops with different rooting depths makes more efficient use of garden space and reduces competition for nutrients. That's why shallow-rooted onions thrive near deeper-rooted squash or beets, for instance. Here are the root characteristics of some common crops, based on research conducted by David Wolfe, associate professor at Cornell University's department of fruit and vegetable science.

You'll find that these characteristics can vary depending on your cultivar selection and soil type;

roots tend to move deeper in sandy soil and stay shallower in heavy or shallow soil. Transplanting can also cause normally deep-rooted plants—like peppers and tomatoes—to form shallower, more branching root systems.

- **Very shallow rooters** (to 18 inches [45 cm] deep): Celery, lettuce, onion, and radish
- **Shallow rooters** (to 2 feet [60 cm] deep): Broccoli, cabbage, cauliflower, Chinese cabbage, cucumber, muskmelon, pepper (transplanted), spinach, and tomato (transplanted)
- **Intermediate rooters** (to 4 feet [1.2 m] deep): Bean (snap), beet, carrot, eggplant, pea, pepper (direct-sown), rutabaga, and summer squash
- **Deep rooters** (to 6 feet [1.8 m] deep): Asparagus, beans (lima), parsnip, pumpkin, tomato (direct-sown), watermelon, and winter squash

Combine Compatible Nutrient Needs

You've probably heard the nursery rhyme about Jack Sprat, who could eat no fat, and his wife, who could eat no lean. This little bit of poetry has a moral that also applies to interplanted gardens. Different plants have different nutrient needs, so you can interplant companions that will each use a particular part of the soil's total nutrient content.

All plants need a certain amount of three major soil nutrients: nitrogen, potassium, and phosphorus. Plants also need minute quantities of minor nutrients, including calcium, magnesium, manganese, copper, and iron. But different crops may draw these elements out of the soil at varying rates. In general, leafy vegetables tend to use more

Squash plants need nutrient-rich soil, so work in plenty of compost before planting for good growth.

Herbs like sage and fennel are light feeders.

nitrogen for lush green growth. Rooting and fruiting vegetables require more potassium and phosphorus to develop vigorous roots and flowers.

Individual crops may have special requirements for particular nutrients. Peppers, for instance, need abundant phosphorus for good leaf color and shape. Cabbage, broccoli, and cauliflower need a ready supply of calcium for good growth. Calcium also helps prevent blossom end rot in tomatoes. Boron, in minute amounts, is necessary for good growth and color in cauliflowers, carrots, beets, and rutabagas. Lettuce needs some copper for good leaf color.

Related plants tend to have similar nutrient needs. Heavy feeders, including plants in the tomato and cabbage families, consume a lot of nutrients. Light and moderate feeders, including plants in the squash and carrot families, use nutrients at a more modest rate. Soil improvers—plants in the pea family—actually help to rebuild nutrient levels by returning nitrogen to the soil.

Feeding Habits of Common Crops

Understanding the nutrient needs of your crops will help you plan the most effective interplantings possible. In general, it's best to avoid combining plants that have similar nutrient needs; otherwise, they'll compete

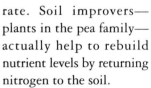

Leeks, onions, garlic, and other onion-family plants tend to be light feeders.

Sunflowers and melons can be good companions if you have fertile soil.

for the available nutrients and both crops will suffer.

If you do need to pair plants with similar needs, at least try to choose ones that have different rooting depths, so they'll scrounge for nutrients in different parts of the soil. (See "Rooting Depths of Common Crops" on page 45 to determine the rooting depths of the plants you want to grow.) Following are the general feeding habits of some popular vegetables and herbs:

- **Heavy Feeders:** Asparagus, broccoli, brussels sprouts, cabbage, cauliflower, celery, chard, collards, corn, cucumbers, eggplant, kale, kohlrabi, lettuce, melons, okra, parsley, parsnips, peppers, potatoes, pumpkins, rhubarb, spinach, squash (summer and winter), sunflowers, tomatoes, and watermelons
- **Light to Moderate Feeders:** Basil, beets, carrots, cilantro (coriander), dill, fennel, garlic, leeks, onions, radishes, rutabagas, sage, salsify, shallots, sweet potatoes, thyme, and turnips
- **Soil Improvers:** Alfalfa, broad beans, clovers, lima beans, lupines (*Lupinus* spp.), peanuts, peas, shell beans, snap beans, soybeans, sweetclovers, and vetches

Combining Compatible Crops

Use your knowledge of plant feeding habits to fine-tune your interplanting plans. Here are some examples of compatible combinations for you to try.

Heavy Feeder with a Soil Improver Try bush beans with eggplant. The beans will flourish while the eggplant is young. When you've picked the first big crop of beans, cut off and compost the stems and let the roots decay to benefit the fruiting eggplant.

High-calcium Feeder with Low-calcium Feeder Since cabbage, cauliflower, and broccoli require a steady supply of calcium, plant them with an unrelated crop that will not compete for this important nutrient. Interplant cabbage with marigolds, nasturtiums, sage, or thyme. Interplant broccoli and cauliflower with beets, nasturtiums, marigolds, or sage. Don't plant high-calcium feeders with tomatoes, which could suffer blossom end rot due to calcium depletion.

Low-nitrogen Feeder with Heavy Feeder Many herbs, including basil, sage, and thyme, produce more fragrant and flavorful foliage if they grow slowly, without the presence of too much nitrogen. If you interplant them in average soil with a heavy feeder, you can create the right lean balance for their growth. Blend basil with peppers or tomatoes. Mix sage with Chinese cabbage, collards, kale, or kohlrabi. Interplant thyme with broccoli or cabbage; try beans with cucumbers, corn, or squash.

Cabbage and its relatives are heavy feeders; try them with light-feeding companions like thyme and onions.

Ornamental and culinary sages tend to be light feeders; rich soil will produce soft growth and fewer flowers.

Think about Light and Shade Tolerance

Any time you put in a plant or install a fence or structure you are creating shade. Trees and shrubs are the most obvious shade producers, but even closely planted flowers and vegetables can shade each other. As you plan your interplantings, you'll have to consider the light requirements of individual crops. Then you will know which to choose for the sunny, exposed places and which for the darker, shadier spots.

Most vegetables and flowers need full sun; some can grow in partial shade. Plants that thrive in full sun, including corn, tomatoes, and beans, usually need 6 hours of direct sunlight or more per day. Plants for partial shade—including lettuce and spinach—can make do with 4 to 6 hours of sun a day. Oftentimes, partially shaded sites are cooler and moister than sunny sites. This provides ideal conditions for leafy and rooting vegetables during warm weather.

Few plants will tolerate deep shade, like the shadow cast under mature maples in summer or the year-long darkness beneath evergreen trees. These sites are best left mulched or planted with tough, shade-tolerant groundcovers like English ivy (*Hedera helix*) and periwinkles (*Vinca* spp.).

Identifying Your Conditions

You can easily tell which parts of your garden have full sun or a half day of shade. As you have time (once a week or so), watch when the sun falls directly on the garden and note the number of hours it lingers. Keep track on your calendar—you'll see the numbers of hours of sun change with the seasons. Then match the average number of hours of sun with the needs of sun-loving or shade-loving species.

If your garden is next to your house, you'll find a big difference between the exposure on north-, south-, east-, or west-facing walls. In an open yard, a garden on the south side of a house will be in full sun all day. The north side will be enveloped in a permanent shadow; it may be bright, but it will never receive direct sun. The east side, which catches mild morning sun rays, will have cool partial to full sun for part of the day. The west side, which receives afternoon sun, can be quite hot with either partial or full sun.

Many herbs, like this French lavender (*Lavandula stoechas*), need full sun to grow and thrive in your garden.

Considering Plant Shadows

Shadows also fall along predictable lines, usually stretching to the north but varying in length depending on the height of the sun at different seasons. A plant's shadow may grow longer as the plant grows taller (again depending on the angle of the sun), and this can affect nearby interplanted crops. In any case, if you put tall plants like corn and Jerusalem

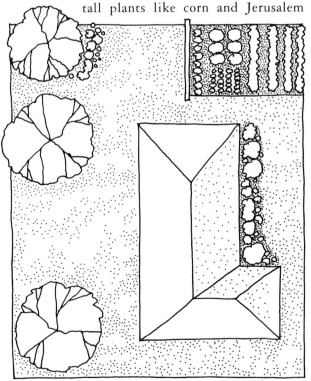

As you choose a site for your companion garden, remember to allow for the shade cast by trees, fences, and buildings. Choose the sunniest spot you have for your vegetables.

Raspberries and most other fruits need full sun for strong, healthy growth and highest yields.

artichokes at the north end of the garden, they won't shade other crops. But if you want to shade a crop from the hot afternoon sun, set a tall plant to the west of it.

Here's another example of how you can use the shadows of growing plants to your advantage. Plant carrots as usual in spring. Once they are up in early summer, plant pole beans on either side of the carrot row and let the pole beans climb sloping trellises that link over top of the carrots. The carrot roots will be getting big when the soil is warm enough to plant the pole beans. The pole beans will take several weeks to climb up their trellis, giving the carrots enough full sun to mature. Once the bean vines have filled out, harvest the carrots. Then plant heat-tolerant lettuce in the shade beneath the sloping trellis.

Light Requirements of Common Crops

Plants that tolerate partial shade are often more vigorous and productive when grown with more sunlight. Following are suggestions of garden plants and companions that are adapted to different light levels:

- **Plants That Need Full Sun:** Artichoke, asparagus, asters, beans, blackberries, broccoli, brussels sprouts, cauliflower, celeriac, celery, chrysanthemums (*Chrysanthemum* spp.), corn, eggplants, goldenrods (*Solidago* spp.), kale, lavender, leeks, melons, mustards, okra, onions, parsnips, peanuts, peppers, potato, pumpkin, raspberries, rutabaga, sage, shallots, squash, strawberries, sunflowers, sweet potatoes, thyme, tomatoes, turnip, watermelon, and yarrow
- **Plants That Tolerate Partial Shade:** Alyssum, arugula, basil, bee balm, beets, broccoli, chard, cabbage, carrots, chervil, cucumbers, endive, kolhrabi, lettuce, lovage, mint, peas, parsley, pansies, parsnips, radishes, rhubarb, and spinach
- **Plants That Tolerate Full Shade:** Browallia, English ivy (*Hedera helix*), hostas, impatiens, lemon balm, lovage, mint, periwinkles (*Vinca* spp.), pachysandra, sweet woodruff (*Galium odoratum*), and tuberous begonias

With a few hours of sun a day, you can grow crops like chard and lettuce, as well as many ornamental plants.

Even in the sunniest garden, trellises and tall plants will cast shade for heat-sensitive crops like lettuce.

CREATING A PLANTING PLAN

Careful planning is probably the single most important thing you can do to ensure a healthy, productive garden of any kind. It is especially critical if you are interplanting or relying on companion planting to help deal with pests. *Before* you order seeds, buy plants, or grab a spade, sit down and put your plans for the season on paper. Start by deciding what you want to grow and how much. Then figure out when you can plant each crop, where you are going to plant it, and what you are going to plant it with.

You'll also need some garden diagrams to help you remember where you put different crops last year and where you should put them this year. When this is done, you'll want to make a couple of tracings or photocopies of your garden plans. (That way you can take one out into the garden with you and won't have to worry when it gets crumpled or dirty.)

No doubt about it—creating a planting plan does take some time and effort. But it is a fun activity for a dull winter day, when you'd rather be thinking about the warm summer to come than staring out the window at yet another day of rain or snow. Plus, the few hours you put in now will save you much more time during the season, when you can follow your plan instead of puzzling about what to plant next.

Only you can decide what to grow or how much—that depends on your own wants, needs, and available growing conditions. But in this chapter, you will find answers to your other planning questions and learn how to put all your information together to create a functional planting plan for your best garden ever. "Basic Planning Principles" on page 52 covers the steps to preparing a garden map and devising personalized planting schedules. "Planning Crop Rotations" on page 54 tells how changing planting sites each year can help control garden pests and diseases, as well as make maximum use of soil nutrients. "Timing Spring Plantings" on page 58 helps you figure out just how early you can start planting seeds and transplants in your area. "Midseason Replacements" on page 60 suggests plants that grow best during the main part of the gardening season. And if you want to extend your harvest into fall, "Late-season Plantings" on page 62 tells you how to get the most out of the season with cool-weather crops.

Creating an effective planting plan is a lot like putting together a jigsaw puzzle. As you create your plan, you'll need to consider factors like soil, light, and nutrient needs, as well as growth habits and life cycles.

Starting with an organized garden layout makes future planning and planting easier.

Basic Planning Principles

If you are interplanting or companion planting, you have a lot of factors to consider as you choose what to grow. Plant heights, life cycles, rooting depths, nutrient needs—they're enough to make your head spin if you try to remember them all. Putting your thoughts on paper will help you create a coherent, functional plan for getting the most out of your garden all season long.

Making a Crop Inventory

Pick a winter day to gather your seed catalogs, notes, paper, and pencils in a spot where you can spread everything out. First make a chart of the plants you want to grow and whether they prefer cool or warm temperatures (see "Cool- and Warm-season Crops" to see which categories your crops fall into). Also include columns for each crop's height, shape, rooting depth, light and nutrient requirements, and time to maturity. See "Spacing Your Plants" on page 72 to determine how much room your crops need. Also estimate how much you want to grow of each.

Now, flip through the "Plant by Plant Guide," starting on page 94, to find which companions will take care of pests, maximize space, or increase soil fertility. Make a note of the appropriate companions by each crop.

Mapping Your Plan

Now that you've made a crop inventory, map your planting strategy out on a scaled drawing of your garden. Let 1 inch (2.5 cm) on your planting diagram equal 5 feet (1.5 m) of garden space so you can include some details. (Graph paper is handy for this step.) Draw in the boundaries of your vegetable garden and the outlines of existing beds, if any. Mark off a place within the garden for planting perennial vegetables, herbs, and flowers if you don't already have such an area. Note north, south, east, and west with any trees or structures that cast shade over the garden. Now, make a number of photocopies of this base map (or make tracing paper overlays), so you can experiment on paper with different crop layouts and record your plans for the season.

Next, cut out construction paper squares, circles, triangles, or rectangles to represent each crop or group of interplanted companions. Use different colors so you can tell them apart easily. Begin by laying out pieces for early-season crops or groupings in the open spaces on the spring garden plan. ("Timing Spring Plantings" on page 58 covers crop suggestions and strategies for getting an early start on the gardening

Mixing plants with different heights and growth habits will give each one room to grow without crowding the others.

Cool-season crops like cauliflower, broccoli, and other cabbage relatives grow best from spring or fall plantings.

Tomatoes need a long growing season, so give them a head start by setting out transplants in late spring.

season.) Now, take another copy of your base plan and arrange the pieces that represent a succession planting of midseason crops in the available spaces. (See "Midseason Replacements" on page 60 if you need specific ideas for summer plantings.) Make a third map for your fall-planted crops (like those suggested in "Late-season Plantings" on page 62).

As you lay out your paper pieces, make sure you allow adequate spacing between crops or groupings, as listed in your crop inventory. If you plan to rotate your crops, consider where you grew each crop the previous year, and choose a different site this year. When everything fits, use clear tape to secure the crop models to the plan so you can refer to them at planting time.

Cool- and Warm-season Crops

Vegetable crops differ widely in their preferred growing temperatures, so it's smart to know their needs before you plant. Set out or sow cool-weather crops a few weeks before the average date of the last spring frost in your area. In warm climates, you can make a late planting of cold-season crops in late summer or early fall to mature in fall and winter. Set out warm-season crops after the last frost (protect them with row covers if a cold snap occurs after planting).

Listed below are some common vegetable crops, grouped by the growing season they prefer.

Cool Season: Beets, broccoli, brussels sprouts, cabbage, carrots, cauliflower, celery, chard, endive, kale, lettuce, lovage, mustard, onions, parsnips, peas, potatoes, radishes, rutabagas, spinach, and turnips

Warm Season: Basil, corn, cucumbers, eggplant, lima beans, melons, okra, New Zealand spinach, peanuts, peppers, pumpkins, shell beans, snap beans, squash, sweet potatoes, tomatoes, and watermelons

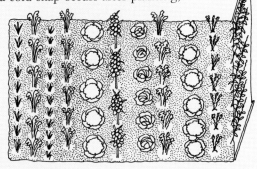

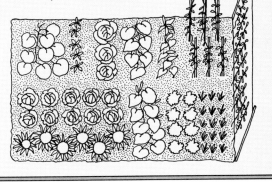

Rotating planting areas each year will help to keep your crops healthy and productive.

Planning Crop Rotations

Crop rotation is the technique of alternating planting sites to protect the soil and minimize pest and disease problems. There are about as many crop rotation systems as there are gardeners who use this technique. If you've never tried crop rotation before, don't be intimidated by the complicated instructions you may have heard—rotation systems can be as simple or as complex as you want them to be. In this section, you'll learn why crop rotation is important, then find three basic rotation systems you can choose from.

Why Bother with Crop Rotation?

Planting crops in different spots each season or year is a great way to minimize many pest and disease problems and maximize soil fertility.

Balancing Soil Nutrients If you alternate growing different kinds of crops in a particular site, you can balance the amount of nutrients that are drawn from the soil. For instance, leafy crops like lettuce and spinach need high nitrogen levels to grow fast and sweet. Root crops, on the other hand, need less nitrogen and more potassium and phosphorus for good root development.

Alternating crops with different needs can help assure that no one nutrient will be excessively depleted during the season.

Improving Soil Conditions You also can rotate crops to condition or improve the soil. Plant strong, deep-rooted crops like clovers to break up heavy or compacted soil and bring nutrients up from deep in the soil. Then work the foliage and roots into the soil; as they break down, they'll add organic matter and nutrients for subsequent crops. Soil-improving crops are a great way to rebuild soil fertility after growing heavy feeders like squash and corn.

Avoid planting new citrus trees where old ones have died; pathogens or allelopathic compounds may linger in the soil.

Legumes like peas and beans can enrich the soil for future crops, especially if you turn the plants into the soil.

Minimizing Pests and Diseases Crop rotation also helps to prevent many soil-dwelling pests and disease-causing organisms from building up to damaging levels. If, for example, your tomatoes are infected with early blight one year, they will likely drop pathogen-carrying leaves on the soil. Those leaves can provide an overwintering site for the disease organisms. If you plant tomatoes or other susceptible plants in that spot next year, the pathogens will be ready and waiting to attack. But if you plant those crops in another part of the garden, the pathogens may die off after a year or two, leaving the site available for a healthy crop of tomatoes again.

Crop rotation for disease control is most effective against short-lived or host-specific pathogens. Host-specific means that a disease will only affect certain types of crops. Club root, for instance, only affects plants in the cabbage family. If your cabbages are affected by club root, you can plant peppers or celery or other nonrelated crops in that spot the following years with no problem. Some diseases, like Verticillium wilt, can attack many different plants or survive in the soil for many years without a host. In these cases, crop rotation is not an effective control.

Weeding through the Options

Crop rotation systems can be simple or complicated. The more factors you take into account, the more complex—and more effective—it gets. But even the simplest crop rotation system is better than none at all. It's often best to start with a simple system and work up to a more complex one as you gain confidence.

Simple System The most basic form of crop rotation is to simply avoid planting the same crop in the same place year after year or season after season. Keep track of where you planted each item the previous season and move it elsewhere next time.

Intermediate System Get a little more advanced by grouping and rotating your crops by plant types: leafy crops, root crops, fruiting crops, and legumes. Leafy plants like cabbage, broccoli, cauliflower, lettuce, celery, collards, and spinach tend to be shallow-rooted and need rich soil. Root crops like radishes, carrots, beets, turnips, garlic, onions, and potatoes usually grow best in loose, average soil where nitrogen is not too abundant. Fruiting crops such as corn, cucumbers, eggplants, melons, peppers, pumpkins, squash, and tomatoes prefer humus-rich soil with balanced fertility. Legumes—including beans, clovers, peas, peanuts, and soybeans—grow in average soil and leave behind nitrogen and soil-enriching

Creating clearly defined planting areas makes garden record keeping and rotation planning a snap.

organic matter when their remains are worked in.

Each time you plant, move these different groups around to make the best use of soil nutrients. You may want to start with leafy crops, followed by root crops, soil-enriching legumes, and fruiting crops; then begin the cycle again. If you have several garden beds, start each one with a different group so you can harvest some of each type of crop each season.

In-depth System To minimize pests and diseases and maximize soil nutrients, you can rotate blocks of plants according to their botanical families. If you're not sure what family your crop is in, try looking it up in "Family Resemblances." Entries in the "Plant by Plant Guide,"

Here's a simple crop rotation system based on four beds. One bed—Plot D—is set aside for permanent crops like asparagus and rhubarb. Each year, the other plantings move to the next bed in sequence (A to B, B to C, and C to A).

Root crops, such as turnips, carrots, beets, and radishes, grow best where the soil isn't high in nitrogen.

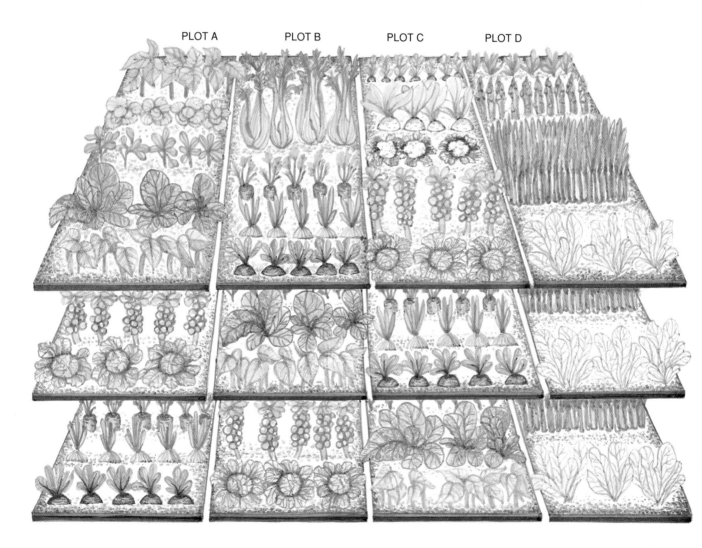

starting on page 94, also give the family name of each plant to the right above the crop's common name.

Here is a sample 5-year rotation cycle that is easy to follow. If you divide your garden up into four blocks, each starting with a different year of this cycle, you can harvest plants from each family at any given time.

- **Year One**: In the spring, work in aged manure and then plant cabbage-family (Cruciferae) crops, like cabbage or broccoli. When those plants are done, work in some compost and plant carrot-family (Umbelliferae) crops like carrots, dill, or parsley for fall harvest.
- **Year Two**: Plant pea-family (Leguminosae) crops like peas or fava beans in spring to enrich the soil. Follow them with heavy-feeding tomato-family (Solanaceae) members, such as tomatoes and peppers.
- **Year Three**: Add more compost and grow a "miscellaneous-family" crop, like chard (Chenopodiaceae) or onions (Liliaceae). Follow with summer plantings of snap or pole beans (Leguminosae) as space permits.
- **Year Four**: Plant a different "miscellaneous-family" crop, such as corn (Gramineae) or lettuce (Compositae). After harvest, or as space permits, replenish the soil with compost and grow squash-family (Cucurbitaceae) members, like cucumbers and summer or winter squash.
- **Year Five**: Begin again with Year One.

Club root is a soilborne disease that attacks cabbage-family plants; crop rotation can help minimize problems.

Family Resemblances

Closely related plants tend to have similar nutrient needs and are quite often susceptible to the same kinds of pests and diseases. The following list explains some similar characteristics shared by members of the major vegetable plant families.

- The tomato family (Solanaceae) includes tomatoes, eggplants, peppers, and potatoes. These plants tend to be heavy nutrient consumers and are prone to many fungal diseases, including Verticillium wilt.
- The squash family (Cucurbitaceae) includes cucumbers, summer and winter squash, gourds, pumpkins, and melons—all moderate nutrient users. They are all prone to cucumber beetles, squash borers, wilts, mosaic virus, and other problems.
- The cabbage family (Cruciferae) includes broccoli, cabbages, cauliflower, collards, kale, kohlrabi, and mustard; also radish, turnip, and rutabaga. Although all are heavy nutrient users, the latter three root crops require less nitrogen. All can be attacked by cabbage maggots, cabbage loopers, and imported cabbageworms, as well as the fungal disease club root.
- The pea family (Leguminosae) includes snap and lima beans, peas, fava beans, runner beans, and green manures like alfalfa, lupines, and vetches. All of these crops help improve the soil by adding nitrogen when they decay. They don't share many problems, although pests can build up if you replant the same crop in the same location repeatedly.
- The carrot family (Umbelliferae) includes carrots, parsnips, parsley, dill, angelica, and Queen-Anne's-lace. These moderately heavy feeders can share nematodes or rot diseases.

Timing Spring Plantings

For most of us, the garden year begins in spring. A sudden spell of warm weather may have your fingers itching to dig and plant, but don't be too hasty—even cool-season crops will not grow in ice-encrusted soil. But if you wait for the right planting conditions and choose the right crops, you can start harvesting weeks before your neighbors

How Soon Can You Plant?

There are two ways you can determine the right planting time for your area: by soil temperature or by the last frost date. Monitor the soil warmth with a soil thermometer, and plant when the temperature is consistently at least 55°F (13°C) but less than 70°F (21°C). Alternately, contact your county's Cooperative Extension Service, farm bureau, or local botanical garden to find out the average date of the last spring frost in your area. Then count back 2 to 8 weeks, depending on the kind of crop you have.

Setting out onions as transplants can speed your harvest by as much as 5 weeks over direct-sown seeds.

spinach, and chicory seeds in moist paper towels enclosed in a plastic bag and set in a warm place. As soon as you see growth beginning to peek out of the seed coat (usually in just a few days), plant the sprouted seeds gently in the garden.

Get an even greater head start by purchasing or growing your own transplants of broccoli, cabbage,

You can plant the hardiest of the cool-weather plants, including lovage, lettuce, chicory, fava beans, and turnips, as soon as the soil is thawed and dry enough to work in spring. Others, such as cauliflower, beets, and peas, should wait until 2 to 4 weeks before the last frost. If the weather seems exceptionally cold, wait a few days or a week to plant—these crops will grow much faster in a cool, rather than cold, soil.

Seeds or Seedlings?

Most early crops, including radishes, carrots, chicory, lettuce, and peas, grow well from direct-sown seed. In fact, this is the best way to handle radishes, carrots, and peas because they respond poorly to transplanting. For a faster start, you can presprout lettuce,

Planting Seedlings

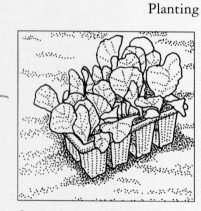

Start with the best-looking, healthiest seedlings you can find.

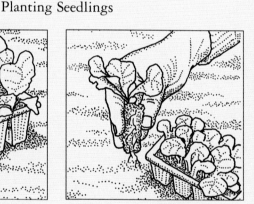

Push up on the bottom of the container to pop out each seedling.

Set the seedlings at the same depth they were growing in the container.

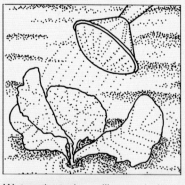

Water planted seedlings to help settle them into the soil.

Presprouting Seeds

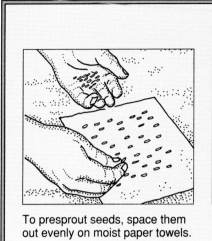

To presprout seeds, space them out evenly on moist paper towels.

Carefully roll or fold up the paper towel to keep seeds evenly moist.

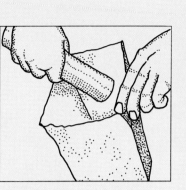

Enclose the towel in a plastic bag; check daily for germination.

onion, chicory, and lettuce. By planting seedlings, you may be able to harvest them as much as 6 weeks earlier than direct-sown crops. "Some Seedling Sense" offers tips on buying and handling transplants.

Companion Planting with Cool-season Crops

Because you have several options for getting your crop in the ground—direct-sown seed, presprouted seed, or transplants—you can easily vary the timing to make companion planting work best. You could, for instance, plant lettuce seedlings with direct-sown cabbage seeds. You'll harvest the lettuce early enough to give the cabbage room to grow.

If you are interplanting to encourage beneficial insects or to trap pests, arrange the timing so both your crop and its companion grow at about the same pace. For example, imagine you want to attract flea beetles away from your Chinese cabbage to a mustard trap crop. Plant several mustard seeds about 6 weeks before the last frost date, and plant additional seeds every 5 days for the next couple of weeks. Give the first mustard planting a week or two to grow and attract flea beetles. Then follow with Chinese cabbage seedlings and destroy infested mustard plants.

Some Seedling Sense

One key to successful companion planting is starting with healthy plants. If you are buying transplants, look for well-nourished, young seedlings. They should have bright green leaves and sturdy, compact stems. Also, look under leaves and along stems for pests. If you find whiteflies, aphids, or other pests, buy your seedlings elsewhere.

Before you set out seedlings that have been grown indoors, give them a period of hardening off to ready them for outdoors. ("Setting Out Transplants" on page 70 explains how to help transplants adjust to cool outdoor temperatures.)

Starting with vigorous, well-rooted, pest-free plants is a key part of developing a naturally healthy garden.

Pull out spring weeds as soon as you spot them to give your young seedlings the best possible start.

Wait until the weather warms up to set out tomatoes, peppers, summer squash, basil, and other cold-sensitive crops.

Midseason Replacements

Once the spring weather turns warm and frost-free, it's time to set out frost-tender crops, like tomatoes, peppers, and beans. You may want to pull out some of the early crops (like radishes and lettuce) that are done producing and follow them with a new crop or companion grouping; this technique is known as succession planting. Or you may want to interplant midseason crops around slower growers like broccoli, brussels sprouts, and carrots. Like spring plantings, these midseason replacements need some attention to get them off to a good start for great harvests.

Following Fast Growers

The simplest way to plant midseason crops is to remove the previous planting and start with an empty bed. This method works best following fast-growing spring crops, like radishes, lettuce, spinach, and mustard. These plantings grow and mature quickly, leaving most of the frost-free growing season available for you to grow another crop.

Tear off peat pot rims to prevent them from drawing water from the soil.

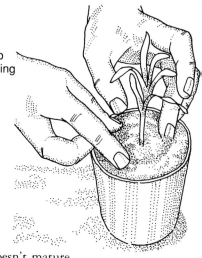

Follow these with slow-maturing or long-yielding tender crops, like tomatoes or peppers.

Replacing Slower Growers

If your spring crop doesn't mature until well into the frost-free growing season, you'll have to follow it or interplant with faster-maturing crops so you can harvest before frost arrives in fall. For example, broccoli, cabbage, cauliflower, and carrots usually produce until the middle of the growing season. Replace them with fast-growing, tender crops such as early corn, bush beans, zucchini, basil, or dill. All of these start easily from direct-sown seed, although you can presprout them or plant young seedlings in peat pots to get a 1- to 2-week head start.

Planning Succession Plantings

The trick to effective succession plantings is choosing crops that will grow and produce a harvest within the space of one growing season. Working out succession plantings is one of the few areas of gardening that can be reduced to numbers. A few simple calculations will give you a good idea if your plans are on the right track.

Determining Maturity Dates For planning successful succession plantings, it's important for you

Once your pea harvest is over, pull out the vines and compost them or turn them under to enrich the soil.

to consider the average number of days to maturity for each crop you're growing. Maturity dates can vary widely by cultivar, so check a seed catalog, the seed packet, or the seedling label to find the average maturity time for your specific crop choices.

Even for a particular cultivar, maturity dates can be different according to different sources. Be sure to check whether the maturity time is from seed to first harvest or from transplanting to first harvest. The maturity dates of tender plants like tomatoes, peppers, and eggplants usually assume that you are setting out transplants. If you plan to grow these plants from direct-sown seed, you need to add 6 to 10 weeks to the maturity time. But if the maturity date is from seed to harvest, you can often shave a week or two off the maturity time by setting out transplants. Squash, cucumbers, and lettuce are just a few of the crops that are available as transplants for gardeners who want to get a head start on the season.

Figuring Out the Frost-free Season The other piece of information you need to know for accurate planning is the length of your frost-free growing season. To determine this, you must know the average dates of the last spring frost and the first fall frost in your area. (Your county's Cooperative Extension Service, farm bureau, or local botanical garden can usually supply this information.) Then count the number of days between the last spring and first fall

While parsley can take the cold, beans and marigolds grow best in midseason, when the weather is warm and settled.

frosts to get the length of your growing season. For example, in Cleveland, Ohio, frost-free weather often stretches between May 15 and October 15, providing an average of 153 frost-free growing days each year.

Putting It All Together As you plan succession plantings, make sure both crops will have time to mature within your frost-free season. Add the maturity times of the succession crops, and include at least 2 to 4 weeks of harvesting time for each crop. Make sure the total doesn't add up to more than the number of frost-free days. If you live in Cleveland, Ohio, for instance, you could easily grow an early crop of lettuce, followed by a midseason planting of tomatoes. But if you wanted to grow a good crop of melons or pumpkins, you wouldn't want to wait until a spring crop was finished—you'd need to set out plants of those slow-maturing crops soon after the frost-free date. (You could also try the tricks mentioned in "Extending the Season" on page 90 to expand your planting options!)

Successive sowings of fast growers like lettuce, planted several weeks apart, can extend the harvest into summer.

Don't forget to thin seedlings according to packet recommendations for best growth.

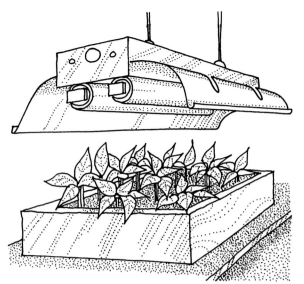

During the heat of summer, start seeds of cool-season crops indoors, perhaps under lights in a cool basement.

Late-season Plantings

You can replace harvested late-maturing spring crops or quick-maturing midseason crops with a fall crop of cool-weather-loving plants, such as cabbage, broccoli, peas, carrots, or lettuce. You'll be planting them during warm weather and letting them mature in the lower temperatures of fall.

Timing Late Plantings

As with midseason plantings, late plantings must have enough time to mature before heavy frosts or snow sets in. If you intend to harvest in the fall or early winter, add about 2 weeks to normal maturity times— as the days get shorter and cooler, plants will not grow as quickly as they do in the lengthening days

Best Picks for Late Planting

Here are a few vegetables, flowers, and herbs that are ideal for late-summer planting.

Annuals: Most plants that thrive in the cool temperatures of spring also adapt well to fall conditions. Cold-tolerant vegetable crops include arugula, beets, broccoli, carrots, kohlrabi, lettuce, mustard, peas, radishes, and turnips. Garlic is usually planted in the fall for harvest the following summer. Among the flowers, try pansies, calendulas, ornamental cabbages, or sweet alyssum.

Perennials: Late summer and early fall can be an excellent time to plant perennial herbs and flowers. Try to plant about 2 months before the first fall frost, to give perennials enough time to form new roots and get established before the soil freezes. Since the weather may be hot when you are planting, be sure to water the new plants thoroughly and often during dry weather, and don't forget to mulch them. Among the herbs, try chives, garlic, oregano, sage, sorrel, thyme, and winter savory. Companion flowers that adapt well to fall planting include asters and chrysanthemums.

Early fall is a great time to plant hardy perennial flowers and herbs into the companion garden.

Set out perennials about 2 months before the first expected fall frost, so they'll get established before winter.

Harden off seedlings in your cold frame before transplanting to the garden.

Early fall is also the ideal time to sow cover crops, like clover and rye, to protect the soil over the winter.

and increasing warmth of the spring. Then count back from the average first fall frost date to determine your planting time. (If you need a refresher on determining maturity dates or frost dates, see "Planning Succession Plantings" on page 60.)

Handling Late-season Crops

Summer heat is a major challenge to getting late plantings of cool-season crops off to a good start. Most frost-tolerant crop seeds will not germinate well in hot weather. One trick is to plant them in a site that is as cool as possible, such as a spot in the shade of tall tender crops. (You could, for instance, plant carrots on the north side of caged tomato plants.) Another technique is to sprinkle the seedbed often with cool water. Or start lettuce or chicory seeds indoors in a cool air-conditioned room or under lights in a basement. Harden off the seedlings by gradually exposing them to longer

periods of sunshine, wind, and warm temperatures before you transplant them into the garden.

Spend a little time replenishing the soil for late season crops—especially if the garden bed has raised two crops before this one. Add some compost as a soil amendment or mulch if you intend to get another harvest out of the area, or plant a green manure crop like clover to reinvigorate the soil for spring.

Help extend your harvest as long as possible by protecting plants with row covers, hot caps, or cold frames. Deep layers of straw, weed-free hay, or other light mulches will protect the soil around root crops like carrots and parsnips, so you can harvest fresh vegetables all winter long. See "Extending the Season" on page 90 for more tips on prolonging crop production well into the cold fall and winter months.

Side-dressing or mulching with compost will help provide extra nutrients for fast-growing fall crops.

A late-summer or early-fall sowing of fast-growing calendulas brightens up the late-season companion garden.

PLANTING COMPANIONS

Once you've decided what crops to grow, what you'll grow them with, and when and where you're going to put them, it's time to put your companion planting system into action. This chapter will guide you through the steps to making your paper plans a successful and rewarding reality.

First, you need to dig in and prepare a productive soil—one that provides all the elements that your plants require to thrive. Plants need soil with a reasonable texture, which is influenced by the blend of different-sized mineral particles and organic matter that compose it. A soil with an abundance of large sand particles tends to drain water well; it stays loose and contains a lot of air (which is necessary for good root growth) but is often dry and low in nutrients. In contrast, soil with a high percentage of clay particles holds plenty of water and nutrients, but it can also be poorly aerated and hard when it dries. Medium-sized silt particles have intermediate characteristics between the two extremes. A loamy soil is composed of a balance of sand, silt, and clay particles and combines the advantages of good drainage with moisture retention.

Unfortunately, there isn't much you can do to change your soil's texture. What you *can* do is improve the soil's *structure*—the way the sand, silt, and clay particles stick together to form clumps (technically known as aggregates). Adding organic matter—in the form of compost, leaves, grass clippings, or similar materials—is the key to improving all kinds of soils. Organic matter helps loosen up tight clayey soils and increases the water- and nutrient-holding capacity of sandy soils.

It also encourages the soil particles to form crumb-like aggregates, which give the soil a loose, crumbly feel and provide ideal conditions for vigorous root growth. "Preparing the Soil" on page 66 explains how to go about starting a new garden plot and how to improve the garden soil you already have.

Once the soil is in good condition, refer again to your garden plan and see where you have decided to plant. Construct raised beds, or lay out single, double, and wide rows. To keep rows and beds straight, line them up with string stretched between two stakes. Use a garden hose to outline circular or free-form planting areas, or mark the edge with a trickle of powdered limestone. "Creating Planting Areas" on page 68 covers many different options for shaping functional garden plots.

Before you plant, check whether your young plants are prepared for the outdoors. If you've gotten your seedlings directly out of a greenhouse or if you've started them indoors under lights, you'll have to take a few days to harden them off. Transplanting your seedlings and sowing seeds correctly—as explained in "Planting and Transplanting" on page 70—will help crops get off to the best start possible.

As you sow and transplant, don't forget to allow your crops enough room to develop to their potential. If you plant too closely or merely scatter seed, plants will clump up and compete for sunlight, moisture, and nutrients. On the other hand, if you leave gaps between plants, you'll waste garden space and encourage weeds. "Spacing Your Plants" on page 72 offers guidelines to help you determine the right amount of room for your crops.

To be successful, companion plantings need the same good care as any other garden. Improving your soil with applications of organic matter before planting is a key step toward getting great results.

Preparing the Soil

Your companion garden needs a rich, fertile soil to be productive and healthy. The time you spend preparing the soil before planting will be amply rewarded by the health and vigor of your crops.

Building Organic Matter

Productive garden soil contains about 5 percent organic matter—fallen bits of plant and animal debris, decaying leaves, and humus. This percentage may seem small, but even a little organic matter can go a long way toward making soil healthy. Decaying organic matter releases nutrients and improves soil structure, creating a loose, crumbly soil that is easy for roots to penetrate. It helps tiny clay particles clump into larger aggregates, improving drainage, and helps hold water and nutrients in normally dry, infertile, sandy soil.

To build up the organic content of your soil, add a 1-inch (2.5 cm) layer of compost or decayed livestock manure each year as an amendment or mulch. You also can substitute a 4-inch (10 cm) layer of coarse organic material such as straw. You'll need to add more organic matter (or make two or three normal applications each year) if you have deep raised beds, extremely heavy or sandy soil, or live in a hot climate, as well as in areas that are cultivated frequently.

Building up soil organic matter is one of the most important steps you can take to ensure healthy, high-yielding crops.

Stirring the Soil

If you are starting a garden in the lawn, strip off the grass with your shovel. Since grass can be full of weed seeds and roots, take the turf strips to the compost pile to decay; you can bring the organic matter back later.

Testing Soil Moisture Once the earth is exposed, dig or till when the ground is slightly moist. The soil is just right if you can squeeze it into a ball and then break the ball up easily with a tap of your finger. If you work the soil when it's too wet, it will lose its nice crumbly structure and cake into brick-hard clods when it dries. If the soil is too dry, it will blow away as dust.

Choosing the Right Tools In a small garden, you can turn the soil with a spade or spading fork. Loosen the soil as much as you can, ideally 8 to 12 inches (20 to 30

Get a Feel for Your Soil

Next time you're out in the garden, take a few minutes to do a simple soil texture test. Wait 2 or 3 days after a drenching rain or thorough irrigation and grasp a handful of soil. Squeeze it into a golf-ball-sized mass. Then shape it into a ribbon by rubbing your thumb against the edge of the ball, so the soil flattens out over the side of your forefinger. If you can squeeze out a 1-inch (2.5 cm) long, slippery-feeling ribbon, you have clayey soil. If the ribbon reaches about ³/₄ inch (2 cm) long before it breaks up, you have a loamy soil. If you can't form much of a ribbon and the soil feels gritty, you have a sandy soil.

Once you've turned the soil and worked in any amendments you plan to add, use a hoe or rake to break up the surface clumps and level the bed for easy planting.

cm) deep. Use a hoe or rake to break up any clumps and form a smooth, level surface.

If you have heavy, clayey soil or a large garden, you may have to rent or buy a rotary tiller. Rotary tillers have churning tines that cut through the soil. A rotary tiller may not let you dig as deep as you can with a spade, but the depth usually is adequate, especially if you plant in mounds or raised beds.

Whenever you cultivate and aerate the soil, you will encourage microscopic soil life to flourish. As the soil microbes increase, they ravenously consume organic matter. So if you turn the soil frequently, remember to add extra compost, aged manure, chopped leaves, or other materials to keep a healthy level of soil organic matter.

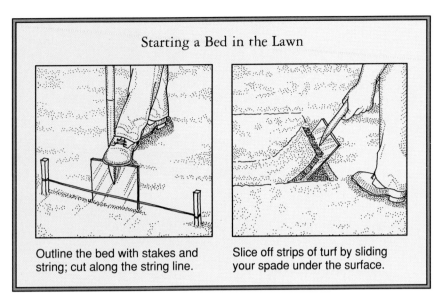

Starting a Bed in the Lawn

Outline the bed with stakes and string; cut along the string line.

Slice off strips of turf by sliding your spade under the surface.

To Dig or to Till

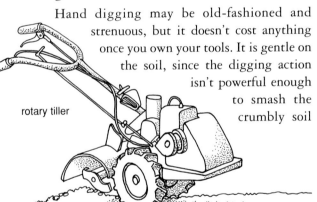

rotary tiller

Hand digging may be old-fashioned and strenuous, but it doesn't cost anything once you own your tools. It is gentle on the soil, since the digging action isn't powerful enough to smash the crumbly soil structure you've been trying so hard to build. And the resulting bed is usually loose enough for most crops, although you may need to do some extra cultivation to prepare a fine seedbed.

Rotary tilling can be easy if you pick a tiller model that is the right size and style for your physique. These machines do consume fuel, and they can be expensive to buy (though renting is also an option). If you till at the right soil moisture level, the resulting fluffy soil is a pleasure to plant in. But tilling when the soil is too wet or too dry can pulverize soil aggregates into a sticky or powder-fine mass. And repeated tilling to the same depth can create a hard layer in the soil that impedes water drainage and root growth.

Which method is best? It really depends on your conditions. If you have a big garden, if your soil is too heavy to dig, or if you don't have the time or energy to hand dig, a rotary tiller may be the right choice. But if you enjoy the feel of preparing the soil by hand, if you have the time and energy, and if you really want to protect your soil's structure, then hand digging may be the way to go. To get the best of both, consider renting a tiller to loosen new soil or fluff up old beds every few years, and hand dig the rest of the time.

Deep digging allows roots to grow and spread easily for water and nutrients, so your crops will thrive.

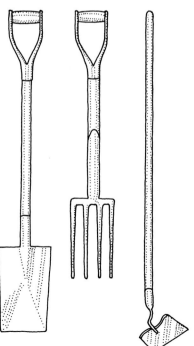

Creating Planting Areas

In a companion-planted garden, you can organize planting arrangements in hundreds of ways. You may choose to interplant repellent or trap companions with your crops, organize succession crops, and intermingle plants with complementary habits. You may decide to create a system of raised beds or to plant in single rows, double rows, hills, clusters, blocks, or wide rows. Each system has its advantages.

Single Rows

Individual rows are good for lanky crops like sunflowers. The open space between individual rows allows for good air circulation and helps reduce fungal diseases on crops like tomatoes. Planting in a single row also allows for enough extra soil to hill around plants like potatoes, celery, and leeks. If you have a small garden, individual rows are not a particularly efficient system; the paths between the rows can take up as much as two-thirds of the available planting space without producing anything.

Double Rows

You can combine two rows side by side (with no path in between) for many kinds of crops, including pole beans, peas, and cucumbers. It is an excellent technique for bush beans, since they will fill out to form a leafy, weed-suppressing canopy. This system is so successful that the same number of bean plants can yield more in double rows than in two separate single rows. Double

Planting in wide rows or blocks is a good option for growing leafy crops like chard, lettuce, and spinach.

rows also are a convenient and effective way to plant climbing crops on either side of a trellis.

You can plant the same crop throughout each row or interplant with companions. For example, in a double row of bush beans, you can slip in 1-foot (30 cm) square blocks of compatible small plants, like beets, carrots, kohlrabi, lettuce, or radishes. The beans help to "hide" the crops in these blocks from pests. Or plant larger 2-foot (60 cm) square blocks of companions like marigolds or summer savory, to confuse pests that will be moving in to attack your bush bean plants.

Wide Rows

Wide rows may span up to 5 feet (1.5 m) across—just wide enough so you can reach the plants in the middle of the row from the path along either side. They can be narrower if your reach isn't quite that long. You'll walk around the bed—not in it—so the soil stays light and perfect for free root growth.

The broad growing area lets you plant several plants in a staggered pattern or side by side across the bed. You can alternate crop plants and their companions. Or you can devote a block of 6 or 8 plants to one crop and a similar block to another compatible crop, repeating the pattern along the length of the row. Adjust planting distances for large or small plants, without leaving spare space for weeds.

Wide rows are great for growing

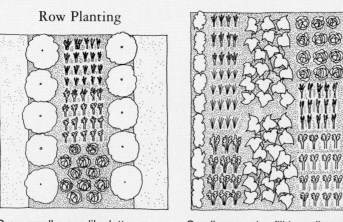

Row Planting

Grow small crops like lettuce between double rows of beans.

Small crops also fill in well around wide rows of spreaders, like squash.

Raking soil into low, flattened mounds is an easy way to make raised beds without formal wood or block framing.

High or Low?

Adjust the height of your garden beds to make the most of your soil and climate. You can plant on level ground or in raised or sunken beds. If your soil is well drained and deep and your climate is mild and moist, simply leave the soil level. But if your soil is shallow or poorly drained, rake the soil into a flat-topped mound 4 to 8 inches (10 to 20 cm) high and 12 to 70 inches (30 to 175 cm) wide. Slope the sides of the mound to keep soil from sliding down with the rain. If you live in a hot or arid climate, you can dig shallow sunken beds, which collect irrigation water and slow its evaporation.

large amounts of small plants like leafy greens and root crops in a small area. Try interplanting leaf lettuce, carrots, radishes, and onions in staggered rows 3 to 6 inches (7.5 to 15 cm) apart in spring. Set about four plants of each kind of crop in 1-foot (30 cm) square blocks to maximize diversity and confuse pests. You also can grow large plants in a wide row. One possible layout would be a 5-foot (1.5 m) wide bed, with a trap crop of nasturtiums along either edge and squash vines at staggered spacing down the middle.

Hills

Hills let you group vining plants like squash in a fertile, raised, sunken, or otherwise improved planting area. The squash vines can spread from there out over the lawn or an unused path. You also can sow four corn seeds each in 2-foot (60 cm) wide hills to encourage wind pollination among plants on the same hill. Leave plenty of room between hills for interplanted crops like cucumbers or squash.

Raised Beds

Many gardeners are beginning to appreciate the advantages of growing crops in raised beds. Since you never walk on the beds, the soil stays loose and fluffy, and yearly cultivation is easy. Planning (especially for crop rotations) is simpler, since the beds are separate, easily identified units that don't change places from year to year. And if your soil is poorly drained or rocky, raised beds can give your crops the extra rooting room they need to succeed.

Building a raised bed can be as simple as raking the soil up into flattened mounds with paths in between. If you want a raised bed that's permanent or taller than 10 inches (25 cm), you'll need to provide extra support to hold the soil. Surround the mounded soil with logs or rocks. Alternatively, you could outline the location where you want the bed with cement blocks, brick, or rot-resistant wood, and fill the frame with good garden soil.

One drawback of raised beds is that they can dry out quickly on hot summer days. The higher they are, the faster they dry. They also can get quite hot. In most cases, beds that are 3 to 5 inches (7.5 to 12.5 cm) high give you the advantages of raised beds without the drawbacks. If you need to make the beds higher, you may need to provide extra mulch and water to crops during summer heat spells.

On sloping sites, terraces act like raised beds, giving you ample growing area for a variety of garden plants.

Planting and Transplanting

Once the soil is ready, it's finally time to start planting! Now you need to learn the best way to plant. The method you use will vary according to whether you are planting seedlings or rooted cuttings, bareroot plants, or hardy, container-grown stock.

Starting with Seeds

Direct-sown seed is an easy and effective way to start many crops, including radishes, carrots, beets, lettuce, peas, beans, and corn. When you sow outdoors, prepare a smooth seedbed so the seeds can have good contact with the soil. Double-check the planting depth on the seed package, then make indentations of the appropriate depth with your finger or a stick. Place one seed at the bottom of each indentation. For wide rows, you can make planting trenches of the appropriate depth and sow the seeds over the area at their appropriate spacing. Then cover the seeds with soil, and pat the soil gently to get good seed-soil contact. Set small seeds like lettuce and carrots, which need shallow planting, on top of the soil, and simply press them in with your hand or the flat part of a hoe. Add a label to remind yourself what the crop is and when you sowed it.

Keep the seedbed moist while the seeds are germinating and afterward when the young seedlings are coming up. Use trickle irrigation or a fine spray

Sunflowers and other large-seeded crops are particularly easy to start by sowing directly in the garden.

Turn container plants over and pull off the pots before planting.

attachment on a hose. Heavy hose blasts can compact the soil or wash it and the seeds away.

Setting Out Transplants

When you buy small plants that have been in a shaded greenhouse, protected showroom, or lath house, find out if they have been hardened off. Hardening off is the process of adapting tender plant leaves to the hot sunshine, drying wind, and less-than-perfect moisture levels of the outside garden. Plants babied in a humid greenhouse or nurtured under lights in your spare bedroom will not be ready for the challenges outdoors. If you move them right out into bright sun, the leaves will burn and turn brown, rather like a winter-weary tourist turns red after spending a day at a Hawaiian beach.

Start hardening off the plants about 1 week before you want to plant them. First, cut back on the amount you water. Don't let the seedlings reach wilting point, but do let the soil dry slightly before you water again. Put the plants in a sheltered shady location—on a breezeway or porch, under a tree, or between your foundation plants. Move the transplants out into the sun for a couple of hours on the first day and a little longer on the second day. Cut back on sun exposure only if the leaves begin to brown or if the plants wilt. After about 5 days, they should be ready for the garden.

If you buy prehardened plants, you can skip this phase and go right to planting. If you have a plant in a peat pot or some other biodegradable container, you can plant it directly in the soil. Peat pots can be slow to decay, so cut slices in the pot or remove the pot bottom for best results. Also tear off the top of the pot so it doesn't extend above the soil and pull water from the rooting area.

If the plant is growing in a container, you need to release the roots gently. Push the root ball out of thin plastic containers by squeezing the pot bottom with one hand while you hold the base of the stem with the other hand. In sturdier containers, put your hand over the pot top (with the stem between two fingers), turn the pot over, pull the base of the stem gently, and tap the pot at the same time to work the roots loose. Now examine the root ball. If the roots are young and loose, you can plant the seedling as is. If the roots are matted, loosen them with your fingers or a knife so they will be able to grow outward instead of continuing to wrap around each other.

Make a hole for the plant in the prepared bed. In most cases, you'll set a young plant in the soil at the same depth at which it is currently growing. (You can set leggy tomato, broccoli, and cabbage seedlings slightly deeper.) Fill the hole with water, gently bring the soil back around the stem, and firm the plant in gently. Label the plant so you can identify it later on.

Handling Other Plants

Most crops and companions are started from seeds or transplants, but you may occasionally buy bareroot plants or get divisions from friends. Plant any bareroot stock as soon as possible. Set the plants on a cone of soil in the planting hole so the crown (the bottom-most stems and leaves) is level with the soil surface. Spread the roots evenly over the cone, firm the soil around the roots, then water.

Divisions are even easier. Set the soil-encrusted root ball in a hole so that the plant sits at the same level it did previously. Firm the soil around the plant and water well.

Fruit trees are usually available bareroot or growing in containers for spring or fall planting.

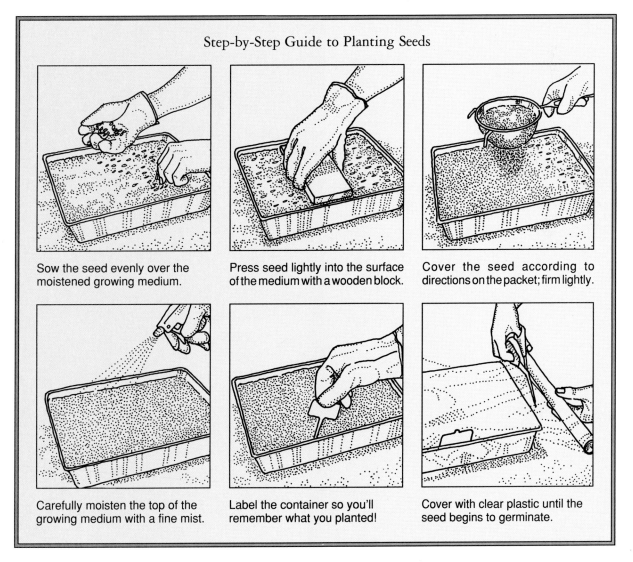

Step-by-Step Guide to Planting Seeds

Sow the seed evenly over the moistened growing medium.

Press seed lightly into the surface of the medium with a wooden block.

Cover the seed according to directions on the packet; firm lightly.

Carefully moisten the top of the growing medium with a fine mist.

Label the container so you'll remember what you planted!

Cover with clear plastic until the seed begins to germinate.

Cabbages may look small at planting, but they'll spread up to 2 feet (60 cm) across by harvest time.

Use the thinnings of leafy or root crops as tender and tasty additions to salads and stir fries.

Spacing Your Plants

Like careful stitches in a needlepoint wallhanging, you need to calculate the proper spacing for each plant so it will fall into the right position in the garden. Perfect spacing lets each plant receive as much sun and root space as it needs, transforming your garden from a bare canvas into a beautiful tapestry of healthy foliage.

Calculate spacing between rows and between plants in a row. Both measurements will vary according to the needs of the crop you plant. When planting in double or wide rows, you can set small plants such as lettuce, onions, and radishes side by side. Bushier plants will have more growing space if you use a zigzag or staggered arrangement. Stagger plants by placing them in one row across from the openings between plants in the neighboring row.

To make spacing easier, stretch out measuring tapes across the length and width of the growing area. Mark each planting spot with an indentation in the soil or spot of ground limestone. For wide beds, buy wire mesh with 1- or 2-inch (2.5 to 5 cm) squares, and stretch it between wooden framing to make a planting guide you can lay on the soil. With 2-inch (5 cm) mesh, for instance, you can plant radishes in every hole or leaf lettuce in every third hole.

Broadcasting: Benefits and Beefs

You can take a casual approach to plant spacing by broadcasting seed over a wide bed or in a row. But seeds, especially tiny ones like herb and lettuce seeds, often bunch up. The result is that several or dozens of plants spring up in one small location. If you are hoping to let those plants grow to maturity, sooner or later you're going to have to make up for the work you didn't do when you planted the seed.

You'll need to thin overcrowded seedlings so the remainders have enough room to develop. (Follow the suggested spacing on the seed packet or in "Some Suggested Spacings.") If you thin

Careful attention to spacing at planting time will pay off later.

Some Suggested Spacings

Crops vary widely in the amount of space they need to thrive. Listed below are the ideal spacings for many common crops.

- **Asparagus:** 24 inches (60 cm) apart in rows 36 to 48 inches (90 to 120 cm) apart
- **Beets:** 2 inches (5 cm) apart in rows 12 inches (30 cm) apart
- **Broccoli:** 12 to 24 inches (30 to 60 cm) apart in rows 24 to 36 inches (60 to 90 cm) apart
- **Bush Beans:** 3 to 6 inches (7.5 to 15 cm) apart in rows 24 to 30 inches (60 to 75 cm) apart
- **Cabbage:** 15 inches (37.5 cm) apart in rows 12 to 24 inches (30 to 60 cm) apart
- **Carrots:** 3 to 4 inches (7.5 to 10 cm) apart in rows about 6 inches (15 cm) apart
- **Chives:** 18 inches (45 cm) apart
- **Corn:** 15 inches (37.5 cm) apart in rows 18 to 24 inches (45 to 60 cm) apart
- **Cucumbers:** 12 inches (30 cm) apart in rows 48 to 60 inches (1.2 to 1.5 m) apart
- **Dill:** 8 to 12 inches (20 to 30 cm) apart
- **Eggplants:** 24 inches (60 cm) apart in rows 24 inches (60 cm) apart
- **Endive:** 12 inches (30 cm) apart in rows 8 to 12 inches (20 to 30 cm) apart
- **Fennel:** 6 inches (15 cm) apart
- **Garlic:** 4 inches (10 cm) apart in rows 12 inches (30 cm) apart
- **Lettuce:** 12 to 16 inches (30 to 40 cm) apart in rows 12 inches (30 cm) apart for heading types; 6 to 8 inches (15 to 20 cm) apart in rows 6 to 8 inches (15 to 20 cm) apart for leafy types
- **Marigolds:** 12 to 24 inches (30 to 60 cm) apart
- **Nasturtiums:** 6 to 12 inches (15 to 30 cm) apart
- **Onions:** 6 inches (15 cm) apart in rows 18 inches (45 cm) apart
- **Oregano:** 18 to 24 inches (45 to 60 cm) apart
- **Peas:** 3 inches (7.5 cm) apart in double rows 8 inches (20 cm) apart, with 36 inches (90 cm) between double rows
- **Peppers:** 24 inches (60 cm) apart in rows 18 inches (45 cm) apart
- **Potatoes:** 6 to 12 inches (15 to 30 cm) apart in rows 10 inches (25 cm) apart
- **Radishes:** 2 to 4 inches (5 to 10 cm) apart in rows 6 to 10 inches (15 to 25 cm) apart
- **Rhubarb:** 48 inches apart (1.2 m)
- **Squash:** 24 inches (60 cm) apart for bush types; 48 inches (1.2 m) apart for vining types
- **Tomatoes:** 12 to 24 inches (30 to 60 cm) apart if plants are trellised; 36 to 48 inches (90 to 120 cm) apart if plants are not trellised

leafy crops when they have a few leaves, you can enjoy them in a salad. If the plants grow faster than you realize, you may have to cut off overcrowded seedlings rather than pulling out the roots. This prevents remaining plants from suffering root damage.

Another problem arises if you try to broadcast several different crops on the same bed. You'll probably find that the faster growers will squeeze out the slower ones. You can circumvent this by sprinkling seed of each crop on its own section of the bed.

If you are interested in harvesting delicate baby greens, now popular as mesclun, broadcasting is an ideal method for you. Harvest the young seedlings when they're only about 4 inches (10 cm) tall.

Proper spacing is especially important for root development—and good yields—in crops like potatoes.

CARING FOR COMPANIONS

Careful planning, thorough soil preparation, and proper planting will get your garden off to a flying start, but your job is not done. You are going to need to shepherd your garden through the growing season to be sure it has what it needs to thrive. You may have to water, mulch, and fertilize to encourage your crops; you might also need to take steps to discourage the pests and diseases that will compete with you for your harvest. And you'll want to make sure you pick at the right time, so you can enjoy the best-tasting produce.

Apart from the care you'd give a regular vegetable garden, successful companion plantings require some extra-special attention throughout the season. When you grow plants so closely together, you'll have to consider how harvesting, fertilizing, or watering one crop will affect its companion. For example, imagine you are interplanting mature cucumber vines on a trellis and lettuce seedlings in the shade below. If you apply some fish emulsion fertilizer to get the lettuce off to a fast start, it may also encourage new growth on the cucumber vines. Both the lettuce and the cucumbers benefit.

But you need to be careful if you interplant crops with different nutrient requirements. Imagine that you interplanted cauliflower and sage in soil that was fairly infertile. If you fertilize liberally to provide extra nutrients for the heavy-feeding cauliflower, the sage (a light feeder) will grow lanky and lose its aroma. You'd have been better off planting both in a reasonably fertile soil and letting the

cauliflower and the sage draw only what they needed.

When dealing with companions, you may want to alter the usual harvest times to benefit remaining crops. For example, if you have interplanted lettuce with cabbage, you may decide to harvest the lettuce a week or two early to give the cabbage extra room. Or, if you have interplanted lettuce and a generous amount of radishes, leave a few of the radishes unharvested and let them flower to attract beneficial insects.

In this chapter, you'll learn all kinds of tips and tricks for providing the special care that companions need. "Watering Wisely" on page 76 tells about different irrigation techniques. "Getting the Most from Mulching" on page 78 covers the different types of mulches you can get and how to apply them. "Fertilizing for Healthy Growth" on page 80 deals with adding a balanced supply of nutrients to meet the special needs of companions. "Recycling Wastes with Composting" on page 82 shows you how to turn garden trimmings and kitchen scraps into a source of free fertilizer and organic matter. Learn about protecting your crops from insects and pathogens in "Dealing with Pests and Diseases" on page 84. "Harvesting for High Yields" on page 88 offers guidelines for picking crops at their peak. Find out how to add some extra time to your harvest with "Extending the Season" on page 90. And when all your crops are harvested, follow the guidelines in "Putting the Garden to Bed" on page 92 to leave the area in good shape for planting the following spring.

You've planned carefully, prepared the soil well, and planted your companion garden—now follow through with regular watering, fertilizing, mulching, and pest control to enjoy your best harvest ever.

Pay special attention to watering during the flowering and fruiting stages of crops like melons, squash, and tomatoes.

Watering Wisely

Water is critical for healthy plant growth. It supports plant tissues and helps the plant stand upright. Water also carries dissolved nutrients from the soil into the plant and provides important materials for the vital process of photosynthesis.

For the most productive growth, your garden plants need a supply of water through the season—either from rainfall or irrigation. You'll know when your plants don't have enough water: The leaves will wilt, flowers will drop off, and fruits, roots, and seeds will become tough or bitter. But like too much of any good thing, too much water can be harmful to plants, drowning roots and providing ideal conditions for the development of rots and other diseases.

For the healthiest plants and highest yields, it's important to know when to water and when not to. One rule of thumb is to apply 1 inch (25 mm) of water a week, either from rainfall or irrigation. In reality, though, this can vary widely through the season, depending on your soil (more frequent irrigation in sandy soil, less in clay) and on the needs of your crops. (See "Be Aware of Water Needs" to find out when some common crops really must have adequate water for the best yields.)

Don't think that a 10-minute session with a hose or a passing afternoon rain shower will meet the water needs of your plants. Brief watering will wet only the surface of the soil, especially in clayey conditions.

What's really important is the amount of water in the rooting zone. To check soil moisture, dig a small hole and look at the soil about 3 to 6 inches (7.5 to 15 cm) below the surface. If the soil there is dry, it's time to water; if it's moist, wait a few days and check again.

Expect to water often if you have tightly interplanted crops, a hot or windy site, sandy soil, or a raised bed. Mulching and enriching the soil with organic matter can help reduce watering needs. Blocking the wind can also cut down on watering by reducing evaporation. In particularly windy areas, block the garden with a hedge, a row of Jerusalem artichokes, or a trellis covered with climbers like scarlet runner beans.

Watering Options

When rainfall is lacking, you'll need to add supplemental water to keep your companion plants growing strongly and producing well. There are many different ways you can apply this water to your garden.

Soaker hoses are a simple but effective way to water your plants without waste due to runoff or evaporation.

Watering by hand may be the only practical option for irrigating small garden plantings.

Hand Watering Watering by hand is most useful for settling in seedlings and irrigating vegetables in containers or very small gardens. It's also a handy way to spot-treat wilting companion plants until you can provide a more thorough watering. Hand watering is not ideal for established plants, since it usually can't supply enough water that will soak slowly into the soil.

Overhead Watering Sprinklers may be among the most common irrigation tools, but they're also among the most inefficient. Most of the water they spray out evaporates, runs off, or falls on weeds and paths. Only a small percentage reaches the crops that really need water. Overhead watering also encourages diseases that spread on the wet leaves.

In hard-to-water spots, consider growing naturally drought-tolerant plants like coneflowers.

Soaker Hoses It's much more effective to provide water at ground level. You can run a soaker hose (which leaks droplets or fine sprays of moisture along its length) next to a single-row planting or between a double-row planting. It will moisten the planting area without benefiting the weeds nearby. You can weave or loop flexible rubber or plastic soaker hoses in and out between clumps of companion plants. Canvas and rigid rubber hoses work best if you lay them in straight lines.

Drip Irrigation If you need greater precision when you water, look into customized drip irrigation systems. These have a network of hoses or pipes, engineered to carry a specific amount of water to any given place in the garden. They use special emitters that let the water seep out to the rooting area of each plant or plant grouping. Be careful if you design this kind of system yourself—it's easy to make a mistake. You can eliminate errors by having a professional design the system based on your garden plan. The designer should be sure the emitters will moisten the entire rooting area of every plant. If they only wet one side, the roots will grow lopsided. When you use the system, make sure you soak the soil deeply, so roots can grow to their maximum width and depth, not clustered in one small area close to the surface.

Drip irrigation is especially helpful for watering container plants.

Be Aware of Water Needs

Most crops grow best with a steady supply of water throughout the growing season but (as with most living things) there are some exceptions. Being aware of your plants' particular needs will enable you to provide the best possible conditions.

Some plants, for instance, will be more sensitive to dry soil during critical times in their life cycles. David Wolfe, from the department of fruit and vegetable science at Cornell University, has identified these critical times for the following crops:

- **Asparagus:** "fern" growth
- **Broccoli, cabbage, and cauliflower:** head development
- **Carrot:** root development
- **Cucumber, eggplant, melon, pepper, pumpkin, squash, and tomato:** flowering and fruiting
- **Peas and snap beans:** pod filling
- **Sweet corn:** tasseling, silking, and ear filling
- **Turnip:** root enlargement

Some drought-tolerant plants are not bothered by less-than-ideal amounts of moisture. Plants that withstand some drought include thyme, rosemary, marjoram, winter savory, sedums (*Sedum* spp.), rose moss (*Portulaca grandiflora*), and coneflowers (*Rudbeckia* and *Echinacea* spp.).

Fallen leaves will provide a wealth of excellent organic material for mulching; best of all, they're free!

Getting the Most from Mulching

Mulching—covering the soil with a layer of organic or inorganic material—can cut garden work in half and significantly improve plant performance at the same time. Mulching minimizes the amount you need to water, the time you spend weeding, and (depending on what you mulch with) the amount you need to fertilize. Mulch also shelters various creatures, including beneficial predatory insects such as ground beetles.

Types of Mulches

There are many different materials you can use for mulching, but they all fall into one of two basic categories: organic or inorganic. Organic mulches, which come from living sources, will break down over time to release nutrients and organic matter into the soil. Compost, shredded leaves, and grass clippings are all examples of organic mulches.

Inorganic mulches, such as plastic, will not improve the soil. But depending on the material you choose, inorganic mulches may keep the soil warmer (or cooler), moister, and less weedy than organically mulched areas. Clear plastic used in hot weather can heat the soil enough to kill off insects and weed seeds (a process known as solarization). Opaque plastic will block the sun and prevent weeds from sprouting. Black and green plastics warm the soil; white plastic keeps the soil cool. Any kind of unperforated plastic blocks air and moisture penetration and encourages shallow root growth. Plastic mulch works well around annuals like squash, cucumbers, and tomatoes, but it is not a good choice around long-lived perennials like asparagus.

Mulching Companions: Dos and Don'ts

Help your companion plants thrive by choosing the right kind of mulches and applying them at the right time. Here are some pointers.

- Mulch large spaces between young squash and to-mato vines with straw or salt hay until you are ready to plant their companions. (At planting time, simply push a bit of the mulch aside to make room for seeds or transplants.)

- Fine mulches like weed-free grass clip-pings are ideal for tight plantings, like between onion bulbs and carrots.

- Mulch heavy feeders—like eggplant, cabbage, and squash—with compost. Put a thin layer of straw, chopped leaves, or grass clippings over the compost to keep it from drying out and crusting over.

- Keep an unmulched zone several inches wide around each plant to prevent crown or root rots and discourage rodents from chewing on the stems.

Thick straw mulch will keep strawberries, squash, and other fruits off the soil, minimizing pest and disease problems.

Suggested Depths for Organic Mulches

Part of effective mulching is applying the material to the right depth. You want to mulch thickly enough to do the job but not so heavily that you smother the soil below.

An inch or two (2.5 to 5 cm) of most mulch materials will slow water loss. But to suppress weeds, you also must block any sunlight from reaching the ground. This requires a thicker layer of organic matter. Here are recommended depths for some common garden mulches.

- **Straw or salt hay:** 6 to 10 inches (15 to 25 cm) deep if loose; up to 3 inches (7.5 cm) if chopped
- **Wood or bark chips:** 3 to 4 inches (7.5 to 10 cm) deep
- **Compost:** 3 to 4 inches (7.5 to 10 cm) deep
- **Shredded leaves:** 2 to 3 inches (5 to 7.5 cm) deep

Black plastic mulch is especially useful in cool-climate gardens, where crops may need a little extra soil warmth.

- Use an organic mulch to moderate soil temperature around cool-season crops (like lettuce, cabbage, and broccoli) that are maturing or germinating in the heat of summer.
- Wait until the soil is thoroughly warm to put an organic mulch on heat-loving crops like eggplants, sweet potatoes, tomatoes, and peppers.
- Apply a thin layer of loose mulch over newly seeded carrots, parsnips, and salsify. The mulch will prevent raindrops from splashing seeds out of the soil and will keep the soil from crusting over (which can inhibit germination).
- Mulch tomatoes to keep roots evenly moist and stop blossom end rot (a disorder that causes the bottom of the fruit to turn black).
- Weed thoroughly before you mulch, or apply mulch before weed seeds emerge to prevent their germination. (You'll still have to pull perennial weeds that grow up through the mulch.)
- If you have cool, damp weather in spring, wait until the soil dries out to mulch.
- If your soil is damp much of the time, be aware that mulch will encourage rots, slugs, and snails. You'll have to weigh the advantages of mulch against the difficulties of controlling these problems.

Coarse bark chips are a good, long-lasting, organic material for mulching pathways and permanent plantings.

Organic mulches will shelter pest-attacking ground beetles.

Good soil preparation will encourage deep rooting, so your plants can search out much of the nutrition they need.

Fertilizing for Healthy Growth

To grow strong, healthy, and productive, your companion plants need a balanced supply of nutrients. Many of these materials are supplied by your soil as organic matter and rock fragments break down and release nutrient-rich particles. But when you're growing plants closely together—as you do for companion planting—it's especially important to make sure there's an ample supply of the necessary materials. When each plant can get the materials it needs, it can grow and yield to its potential. You can supply these extra nutrients by applying the right fertilizers.

Do You Need to Add Fertilizer?

The amount of fertilizer your crops will need depends a good deal on the natural fertility of your soil. Healthy, fertile soil that's rich in organic matter may only need a small application to give plants the extra boost they need. Some soils are lacking in one or two specific nutrients; others may generally be nutrient-poor.

The need for supplemental nutrients also depends on the crops themselves. Plants like thyme, sage, and cosmos grow better on lean soils, without the addition of extra nutrients. Others, like corn and tomatoes, are heavy feeders that may deplete even nutrient-rich soils. Long-established perennials like rhubarb and asparagus can deplete the surrounding soil and may need supplemental nutrients. Closely interplanted crops or crops planted in succession (one after another) also may need extra attention to fertilization.

If the plants you have now seem to be growing well, you may want to assume that the nutrient levels are fine and just apply a complete (balanced) fertilizer to particular crops according to package directions. You can see when plants need extra attention to fertilizer—they may grow slowly, have discolored leaves, or fruit and flower poorly. You also should watch for

Working in ample amounts of compost will help enrich the soil, providing ideal rooting conditions for most crops.

Excess nitrogen encourages plants like nasturtiums and tomatoes to produce leafy growth at the expense of flowers.

signs of too much fertilizer. This can make plants grow overly tall, without fruiting and flowering.

If your plants aren't growing as well as you expect, or if you really want to get the best start in a new garden, it's a good idea to get a soil sample tested by a professional laboratory. Your local Cooperative Extension Service can provide instructions for taking a soil sample and mailing it to the right place. Ask the lab to supply recommendations for organic soil amendments, in case your soil is deficient in nutrients.

Organic Fertilizer Materials

Organic fertilizers are nutrient sources derived from natural products, like animal manures or rock powders. Complete fertilizers contain the major elements required by all plants—nitrogen, potassium, and phosphorus— and sometimes minor elements as well. The labels of packaged fertilizers will display a series of three numbers, which correspond to the percentages of nitrogen (N), phosphate (P), and potash (K). Most organic fertilizers have low numbers, like 5-3-3; a few (such as nitrogen-rich bat guano) may have a ratio as high as 10-3-1. A balanced fertilizer is usually a blend of different materials, to create a product with a fairly even ratio, such as 4-6-4 or 3-3-3. Many fertilizers sold as "natural" aren't completely organic. One way to check is to add

up the three numbers; if they total 15 or less, you're fairly sure the product has organic ingredients.

Specialty fertilizers usually contain only one or two elements. Use

Apply a light dose of solid or liquid fertilizer when plants begin to flower or set fruit.

them to correct a specific nutrient deficiency. If nitrogen is lacking, for instance, you may want to apply bloodmeal (11-0-0) or fish emulsion (5-3-3). Rock phosphate (0-3-0) is a common source of phosphorus, while granite dust (0-0-4) and greensand (0-0-7) are both good organic sources of potassium.

When applying any fertilizer, remember that too much is as bad as (or even worse than) too little. Follow the suggested application rates on the package, or adjust the rates based on the results of your soil test.

How to Apply Fertilizer

If you need to add fertilizer, you have several ways to apply it. Solid (also known as dry or granulated) fertilizers are easy to spread evenly over the soil surface by hand or with a mechanical spreader. Work in solid fertilizer as you're preparing a bed for planting, or scratch it into the soil along rows or around the base of individual plants. For a faster response, apply liquid fertilizers—like seaweed extract or fish emulsion—to the soil around crop roots, or spray them onto plant leaves (a technique called foliar feeding).

When you actually apply fertilizer depends on your crops and the materials you're using. Work dry fertilizer into a bed before planting, or scatter it around the base of perennials in spring. Give young seedlings a boost at transplanting time with a liquid fertilizer like fish emulsion. Later in the season, use a light application of either dry or liquid fertilizer when they begin to flower and produce fruit.

Treat established perennials and shrubs to an application of dry fertilizer in spring; scratch it into the soil.

Recycling Wastes with Composting

One of the keys to a successful companion garden is rich, fertile soil. And one of the best materials you can use to build that soil is compost. Its organic matter conditions the soil, increasing air and moisture content and improving drainage in wet or sticky soils. It's an excellent free source of plant nutrients and mulch. And composting is a great way to recycle grass clippings, leaves, kitchen scraps, and other organic wastes that might otherwise take up space in a landfill.

Making compost can be as simple or as involved as you want it to be. Once you know what ingredients to use and the different ways you can compost, you can choose the method that's best for you.

Compost Ingredients

Just about any kind of organic material can have a place

Used as a soil amendment, mulch, or fertilizer, compost can help all of your companion plantings thrive.

in your compost pile. Green or soft plants and barnyard manure add the vital element nitrogen, which speeds up decomposition and gets the decay process cooking. Woody or fibrous plant debris like brown leaves, wood shavings, and straw provide the necessary carbon-rich material that decomposers feed on to release nutrients and organic material.

What can't go in the pile? Diseased or insect-infested plants and seedy weeds are not good ingredients, unless you plan to use a "hot" composting system. Pests, disease spores, and weed seeds may survive the "cold" composting process and spread throughout your garden as you spread the finished compost. Don't add meat, bones, fats, or oils—they break down very slowly and can attract animals. And avoid adding cat or dog droppings; pet manure may carry diseases that can spread to humans.

Choose a System

You have many options for processing yard debris into compost. They vary in speed and effort. Here is a summary of your options.

Hot Compost Hot composting can give you finished compost in just a few weeks, but it does take some work. You must blend the right balance of ingredients together to create a perfect environment for decay-causing organisms. Alternate layers of high-

---

Enclosing Your Compost

It's not essential to enclose composting areas. You can simply heap garden leftovers up in a pile or spread them over empty garden beds to rot in place. But if you want to keep your compost neatly contained, you can enclose your pile in a bin. Commercially available barrels and bins look nice—some specially designed units may even help speed up the composting process—but they can be expensive to buy. You can build your own three-sectioned bin with chicken wire tacked to lumber framing. Make sure each section is about 3 to 4 feet (90 to 120 cm) high, wide, and deep. Devote one bin to aged compost that is ready to use, another to half-cooked compost, and the last to accumulating fresh yard scraps.

Making Fast, Hot Compost

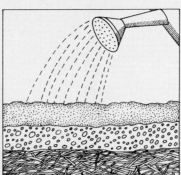
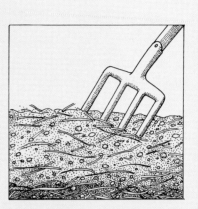

1. Build your compost heap with equal amounts of high-carbon and high-nitrogen materials; add in layers or mix them up.

2. As you add new materials, sprinkle them with a watering can to keep them moist and to encourage decomposition.

3. Aerate the compost pile by turning it once every couple of days using a garden fork. This hastens the microbial activity.

nitrogen and high-carbon debris, or just mix approximately equal volumes together to create a pile about 3 to 4 feet (90 to 120 cm) high, wide, and deep. As you build the pile, add water to make the materials evenly moist but not wet (about the feel of a damp sponge). If you add mature weeds or pest- or disease-infested material, make sure you put them in the center of the pile, where they should be killed by the heat.

Within a day or two, the pile will begin to feel warm. When the pile is hot, turn or fluff it with a pitchfork to mix the ingredients and add oxygen. Turn the pile every few days or weeks to help speed the decomposition process. The compost is ready to use when it is dark and crumbly and when the original materials are unrecognizable.

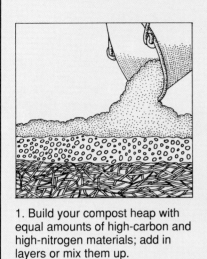

Cold Compost If you have little time or energy for composting, and if you don't mind waiting for results, a cold compost pile may be the thing for you. Make a similar blend of ingredients, but don't worry about keeping the pile moist or turning it. The materials will slowly break down without generating much heat. Cold compost piles can take a year or more to break down garden waste, so start a new pile every year so that you do not hide your finished compost under new debris. Although cold composting takes less work, it doesn't heat up and destroy pests. And since the pile sits longer, rain can wash nutrients out of uncovered compost.

Other Options If you can't make as much compost as you need, you may be able to buy or pick up bulk loads of compost from a community composting or recycling program. Check with your local city hall to see if your area has a composting facility.

Using Compost

Compost is a terrific material for improving your garden soil. Work in a 1- to 2-inch (2.5 to 5 cm) layer into garden beds each spring before your first plantings. Heavy-feeding crops like tomatoes and cabbages also appreciate a compost mulch during the season. Compost will provide a small but balanced supply of nutrients, making it a great amendment for all kinds of companion plantings. It also makes a good liquid fertilizer. Soak a shovelful of compost in a bucket of water; strain, dilute to a light brown color, and spray on plants.

Choose an unused spot close to the garden for your compost; build a loose heap or enclose the material in a bin.

Dealing with Pests and Diseases

Controlling pest damage is one of the major reasons many gardeners try companion planting in the first place. Companion combinations take advantage of natural systems to combat pests by grouping compatible plants that can repel insects, mask crops, or attract beneficial insects. But since so many factors can influence the success of your companion plantings, it is likely that a few pest or disease problems will still pop up in some part of your garden. In this section, you'll learn some easy ways to deal with common problems you may encounter among the companions.

Be a Super Scout

At least once a week, when you have a few spare minutes, wander through your garden. Look for holes, spots, injured stems, deformed leaves, or damaged flowers or fruit. Examine the growing tips of plants for tiny pests like aphids, thrips, or leafhoppers; look closely along stems and under leaves for caterpillars, borers, or spider mites.

If you find a few plant-eating insects around the garden, leave them to be food for insect predators and parasites. But keep an eye on pest population sizes so you'll see if they are getting out of hand. You'll know pests are a problem if their numbers are growing and their feeding is heavy enough to damage plants. Even small numbers of insect pests can be destructive if they carry diseases. Leafhoppers and aphids spread plant viruses; striped and spotted cucumber beetles spread bacterial wilt disease.

Pruning off infested plant parts can be an effective control.

While you are inspecting for pests, keep an eye out for diseases, too. Look to see if any onion bulbs are

Indoors or in a greenhouse, yellow sticky traps can be a useful control for whiteflies, aphids, and fungus gnats.

growing overly soft; check whether black leaf spots are spreading upward on your tomatoes. Some diseases—such as the sooty mold that grows on aphid droppings—are fairly benign. Others can spread quickly and destroy an entire crop.

Make the Right Diagnosis

The key to picking an effective control is knowing what pest or disease you're dealing with. Look in a reference or general gardening book to help you correctly identify the problem. If a book is not enough and you need outside help, contact your county Cooperative Extension Service or local botanical garden. Some large landscaping services also have diagnostic laboratories.

Pick an Appropriate Control

Once you know what you're dealing with, do a little research to identify the most effective and least toxic cure. If an insect is the culprit, learn about the pest so

Handpick snails or trap under boards; check traps daily and destroy pests.

Soap sprays or homemade garlic sprays can be effective against aphids.

Deter slugs by surrounding plants with barriers of diatomaceous earth.

Spray Colorado potato beetle larvae with the biological control BTSD.

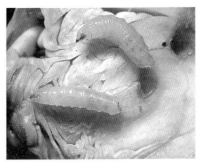

Prevent cabbage maggot damage by protecting plants with row covers.

Handpick caterpillars, or spray with the biological control BT.

you can key in on its weak areas—certain times in its life cycle when it is most susceptible to treatment. Find out what beneficial insects prey upon it and what companion plants can deter or trap it. When you have researched your options, you can decide how to proceed without damaging the interplanted harmony you have already created outdoors.

Cultural Controls An easy and effective way to correct up to 90 percent of disease and pest problems is to change the way you're growing plants. For example, if you have squeezed a plant that prefers full sun into a lightly shaded nook (or interplanted too tightly between taller plants), it can be weakened and unable to resist pest and disease attack. Be sure to keep sun-loving plants, like sweet potatoes, eggplants, and melons, in sunny locations. Give plants that are prone to rot—including onions and peas—well-drained soil. Species susceptible to foliage diseases, including tomatoes, lettuce, and beans, need good air circulation. You also can avoid regular disease problems by buying disease-resistant species and cultivars.

Also, double-check your maintenance methods. Don't nick plants with your hoe or rake: Wounds are an open invitation for pest and disease attack. Stay out of a planting when the foliage is wet so you won't spread diseases as you brush past plants. Plant companions at the proper spacing to let air circulate freely through the remaining foliage and make conditions less desirable for fungal diseases. Proper spacing also avoids

competition for water and nutrients, so plants will naturally be stronger and healthier.

Barriers and Traps Surround plants that are attacked by creeping pests (such as slugs and snails) with sharp or irritant products like diatomaceous earth, lime, or crushed seashells. Dried hot peppers, ground up and dusted on and around onions, carrots, or cabbages, can repel root maggots. Cover plants that are routinely attacked by flying insects or their larvae with lightweight-fabric floating row covers. (Row covers are a great way to protect cabbage-family plants from

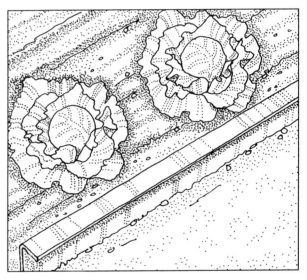

Repel slugs and snails from companion plantings by surrounding raised beds with copper barrier strips.

To prevent frost damage, cover plants when cold weather is predicted.

Pruning for good air circulation can minimize fruit rot problems.

Water and mulch plants during dry weather to prevent leaf scorch.

cabbageworms and loopers, for instance.) Surround beds with copper strips to shock snails and slugs away. Protect small seedlings with cutworm collars—2-inch (5 cm) cardboard tubes you slip over seedlings and push halfway into the soil. Hang yellow sticky traps from stakes near indoor plants to draw and trap aphids.

Handpicking Occasionally you'll have to return with stronger medicine to handle a particular pest or disease problem. You can physically pick off the pests, their egg masses, or disease-spotted leaves. Crush pests or drop them in a bucket of soapy water; put diseased leaves in the center of a hot compost pile or dispose of them in household trash.

Biological Controls Choosing companions that will attract beneficials is a good way to start encouraging native populations of beneficial insects. If the existing beneficials aren't enough to deal with a problem, you can buy more through mail-order garden suppliers. You can purchase enough for a single release, or—for pest problems that tend to hang around—get timed releases sent periodically through the growing season.

Like your native beneficials, these imported good guys will stick around longer if you supply them with pollen- and nectar-producing flowers, such as daisies, lemon balm, thyme, cosmos, catnip, dill, and calendulas.

You also can handle some pests with insect-specific diseases. These diseases attack the nuisance pest without harming plants, beneficial organisms, or animals. Try BT (*Bacillus thuringiensis*), a

---

Herbal Sprays

Many aromatic herbs contain compounds that make them useful pest repellents. To get the full benefit of these compounds, you may need to prepare herbal sprays. Blend 1 to 2 cups (3 oz/90 g to 6 oz/180 g) of dry leaves or 2 to 4 cups (3 oz/90 g to 6 oz/180 g) of fresh leaves with 2 to 4 cups (16 fl oz/500 ml to 32 fl oz/1l) of water; let sit overnight and strain out the herbs. Add 2 to 4 more cups (16 fl oz/500 ml to 32 fl oz/1 l) of water, plus a few drops of liquid dish soap, then spray plants. Try tansy sprays to repel squash bugs or chamomile sprays to protect seedlings from damping off; experiment with other plants.

---

bacterial disease of caterpillars, as a spray or dust to control imported cabbageworms, cabbage loopers, hornworms, gypsy moths, and similar pests.

Last Resorts If less-extreme pest controls don't work, you can call on soaps and botanical insecticides. These products break down quickly after use, so they don't linger long in the environment, but they still can harm beneficial insects and animals if not used carefully. Read the label and apply the spray or dust according to package directions. Treat only troubled plants—not

Adult lacewings feed mostly on pollen and nectar, but their larvae are voracious predators of aphids and other pests.

Fast-moving ground beetles prey on slugs, snails, and other soil-dwelling pests; they're mostly active at night.

the whole crop or bed—preferably in the evening when honeybees have gone home. Try not to spray flowers, which may be visited by predatory wasps. Wait the full period indicated on the label before harvesting vegetables, fruits, or herbs for eating or storage.

If plants are infected with disease, your control choices are fairly limited. Many gardeners have reported success with using a baking soda (sodium bicarbonate) spray against fungal diseases, like powdery mildew. Make a solution by dissolving 1 teaspoon of baking soda in 1 quart (1 l) of warm water. If desired, add up to 1 teaspoon of liquid dish soap to help the solution cling to foliage. Use a spray bottle to wet both tops and bottoms of leaves thoroughly. For seriously infected plants, the best course is usually to remove them before the disease spreads further. Place them in the center of a hot compost pile or dispose of them with household trash.

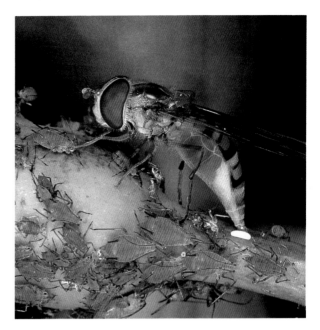

Hover fly larvae are important aphid predators; each one can eat approximately 400 aphids during its development.

If All Else Fails

If pest problems get out of control, protect companion crops by spraying or dusting with one of these materials. Follow package directions on commercially available products.

- **Superior oils** are suitable to use during the growing season on many plants. They coat the foliage, killing aphids, mealybugs, mites, and scale. Superior oil sprays can also discourage some fungal diseases.

- **Insecticidal soap** will kill a wide range of soft-bodied insects, including aphids, spider mites, and thrips. Buy a commercial product, or make your own soap spray by mixing 1 to 3 teaspoons of liquid dish soap in 1 gallon (4 l) of water. Insecticidal soaps can harm some plants, like beans and cucumbers. Before treating a whole plant, test the spray on a few leaves and wait a few days to see if damage appears. Also use caution if applying sprays around sensitive companions. Repeated use of soap sprays can harm plants, so use them only when really necessary.

- **Garlic oil extract** can control many insects and also may have antifungal properties. Soak 3 ounces (85 g) of minced garlic in 2 teaspoons of mineral oil for 24 hours. Strain out the garlic and add 1 pint (600 ml) water

and 1 teaspoon liquid dish soap to the remaining liquid. Mix thoroughly. Spray plants with a solution of 1 to 2 tablespoons of soap mixture and 1 pint (600 ml) of water. This spray can also kill beneficial insects, so only apply it to infested plants.

- **Botanical insecticides** are harvested from plants that contain repellent or toxic compounds. Pyrethrin, an insect nerve poison that affects chewing and sucking pests, can be extracted from pyrethrum daisies (*Chrysanthemum cinerariifolium* and *C. coccineum*). Ryania, derived from a tropical shrub of the same name, is a broad-spectrum insecticide that also is toxic to animals and aquatic life. Rotenone, found in 65 different plant species, works on insects with chewing mouths (like beetles). Sabadilla, derived from a Venezuelan lily relative, attacks beetles, caterpillars, bugs, and thrips; it's also moderately toxic to mammals. Neem, extracted from the seeds of the neem tree (*Azadirachta indica*), can control a wide range of pests and is almost nontoxic to mammals and beneficial insects.

Regular picking will encourage crops like beans, cucumbers, and squash to keep producing new fruit.

Harvest whole heads of lettuce by cutting them off at the soil level when they feel firm to a light touch.

Harvesting for High Yields

After you've put all that effort into planning, planting, and caring for your companions, you deserve to have the best harvest ever. Knowing when and how to pick each crop at the peak of flavor will help you get the best-tasting and highest-quality produce.

Harvesting How-to

Each time you plant a crop, mark the expected maturity date on your calender. About a week before this date, start checking the crop for signs of ripeness. The actual date you'll start harvesting can vary widely, depending on weather conditions that may have quickened or slowed plant development.

Some crops—like sweet corn and bush beans—have a short period in which the produce is at its peak. Others, including carrots, leeks, potatoes, and onions, can be harvested over a period of weeks or months. In most cases, you

For best flavor, wait until melons are fully ripe before you pick them.

shouldn't worry about picking crops too early. In fact, young fruits and leaves are often more flavorful than older produce. Tomatoes, melons, and winter squash are a few exceptions to this rule—their fruits should be fully ripe for best flavor. When in doubt, pick a leaf or fruit and see how it tastes.

Harvest your crops in the morning, after the dew has dried but while the plants are still cool. Pick carefully to avoid damaging the plant and bruising the produce. Keep harvested produce in a cool, shady place until you are ready to use or store it. Brush off any clinging soil, and pull off any bruised or damaged parts before storing.

Special Companion Harvesting Tips

Space your plants carefully and time your harvest so you avoid root damage when you are pulling out interplanted leafy or rooting vegetables. When you uproot a large radish growing next to a tiny carrot seedling, the carrot is bound to suffer. Thin some plants—even harvest some a little earlier than usual—to give ample growing space to later crops.

Instead of uprooting leafy crops such as lettuce or spinach during harvest, snip off whole plants and leave the roots below ground. Then you won't disturb neighboring root systems. Do the same when you remove the plants of fruiting crops—like peas and beans—after harvest.

If you are relying on a fragrant herb to mask or repel pests, harvest from it lightly and often. That helps release some of the fragrance and encourages the herbs to produce more growth.

Handy Harvesting Guidelines

Exactly when you pick for best flavor will vary, depending on the crop and your tastes. Here are some

Pick small potatoes as needed after plants start to flower, or wait until the vines die to harvest full-sized tubers.

basic guidelines for harvesting common crops.

- **Beans, snap:** Cut or break off pods while they are young, tender, and crisp.
- **Beets:** Pull or dig plants when roots are 1 inch (2.5 cm) or more in diameter.
- **Broccoli:** Cut off the main head before the yellow flowers open. In cool weather, smaller sideshoots often develop above the remaining leaves.
- **Cabbages:** Cut heads when they feel tight and firm. Harvest early crops high on the stem to get an extra harvest of tiny heads.
- **Carrots:** Pull or dig roots at any size once they start to develop full color.
- **Cauliflower:** Cut off the white, purple, or green heads (depending on cultivar) before the buds begin to separate.

- **Corn:** Snap off sweet corn ears when the silks have turned brown and dry and the ear feels full. The kernels should be plump and contain sweet milky liquid.
- **Cucumbers:** Harvest pickling cucumbers when they are 3 to 4 inches (8 to 10 cm) long; pick slicing types when they reach 6 to 8 inches (15 to 20 cm) but before they begin to turn yellow.
- **Lettuce:** Remove individual leaves of any size as needed; harvest heads at soil level when they are firm to a light touch.
- **Muskmelons:** Pick muskmelons when they are slightly soft and aromatic and when the fruit slips easily from the vine.
- **Onions:** Pull scallions and onions for fresh use as needed. For storage onions, wait until the foliage yellows; then pull the onions and let them dry in the sun for about a week.
- **Peas:** Cut snow peas from the vines when the pods are perfectly flat; for snap peas, wait until the pods are rounded but still smooth. Pick shelling peas when the pods are plump and the peas are tender.
- **Peppers:** Harvest sweet and hot peppers when they are large enough to use. Or leave them to mature on the plant; they taste fruitier or hotter if you wait.
- **Spinach:** Remove individual leaves of any size; or cut off the entire loose head at ground level.
- **Squash:** Cut summer squashes from the vines when they are small—about 4 to 8 inches (10 to 20 cm) long. Pick winter squash when the shell is hard enough not to be dented by a fingernail.
- **Tomatoes:** Pick when the fruit is evenly colored but still firm.

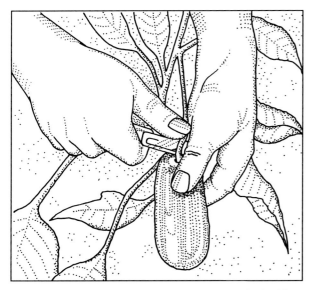

Clip or cut eggplant fruit with some stem attached while the skin is purple and still glossy.

Harvest aromatic herbs lightly and often to release their fragrance and keep plants producing fresh new growth.

Cool-season crops like cabbage and lettuce adapt equally well to either early spring or early fall planting.

Extending the Season

There's nothing quite like the taste of freshly picked produce. And with careful planning, you can enjoy the bounty of your companion garden for up to twice as long each year. Getting an extra early start in the spring, and prolonging the harvest well into fall, takes some work, but that crisp, tasty salad of just-picked produce on your Easter or Thanksgiving table will make it all worthwhile.

Extending the growing season in your companion garden really takes a three-pronged approach: selecting the right plants for the conditions, planting them at the right time, and shielding them from the cold spring or fall temperatures.

Picking the Right Plants

As you choose the plants you want to grow, look for cultivars that are suited to extra-cold conditions. For late-summer and fall crops, check out the array of winter-keeping cultivars of cabbage, lettuce, and beets. 'Springtide' Chinese cabbage, corn salad, 'Easter Egg' radishes, and 'Tyee' hybrid spinach are good choices for early spring. Traditional cool-season crops, like spinach, endive, escarole, broccoli, carrots, chives, and kale, are natural choices for either early-spring or fall growing.

Planting at the Right Time

To start extra early in spring, prepare the soil on a well-drained site in fall. Two weeks before you plant, heat the soil by covering it with green or black plastic. Plant thoroughly hardened-off seedlings or presprouted seeds through slits or holes cut in the plastic.

To harvest in late fall or winter, plant crops in midsummer to late summer. You can sow fast-growing crops like lettuce, spinach, and radishes every 2 weeks, up to 2 weeks before your first fall frost date if you protect the young plants. Plant beets and carrots about 65 days before the first fall frost. If the weather becomes too cold for good growth, plants such as parsley, Swiss chard, chives, and endive can go dormant and then reemerge to grow first thing in spring.

Using Frost Protectors

If cool-season crops will be growing in weather colder than about 40°F (4°C), they'll do better with some

Trellises help protect crops from cold breezes. For extra protection, drape row covers over crops during cold weather.

For a successful onion crop, check catalog recommendations for cultivars that are suited to your growing season.

Wallo'Water protectors can shield young plants from spring frosts.

form of protection. Protective devices also will prevent frost-tender peppers, pumpkins, and other long-yielding summer crops from being damaged by an early frost or two. Surround the plants with hay bales or trellising and drape burlap over them at night or during short cold spells. When Indian summer returns, these tender plants may be able to finish maturing their fruits.

Use smaller enclosures to protect young plants in early spring or late fall. Cover them with a floating row cover, which will help keep the air around the plants a few degrees warmer than the surrounding environment. For better insulation, you can surround individual plants with Wallo'Water protectors, which absorb heat in the daytime and release it slowly at night. Or make a substitute by filling 2-liter plastic soda bottles with water and setting them in a circle around plants.

You also can cover plants with plastic jugs that have the bottom removed, plastic umbrellas, or plastic tunnels stretched over wire hoops. These "minigreenhouses" can hold in too much heat during a warm sunny day, so be prepared to provide some ventilation. Take the cap off the jug, tip the umbrella up on its side, or cut ventilation holes in the tunnel sides.

Cold Frames For a permanent place to protect plants during cold seasons, build a cold frame. The

Fast-growing, cold-tolerant beets are a great choice for either spring or fall growing.

simplest type of cold frame is a bottomless, box-like structure. A good size for a frame is about 4 feet (1.2 m) long and wide. You can make the sides out of cement blocks, wood, or clear fiberglass. Build the back taller than the front, so the lid will sit at about a 45-degree angle. At its lowest point, the frame should be tall enough so plants can grow without touching the roof.

Top the frame with a lid of clear plastic, fiberglass, glass, or Plexiglas that the sun can shine through. You may want to hinge the lid to the back of the frame so you can swing the lid open when you need to reach the plants. Or you could let the lid sit on the frame and slide the lid open.

Set the frame on a level, well-drained, south-facing site. On warm days, prop the lid open with a stick, or invest in mechanical ventilators that open or close the top at a certain temperature or time. Set pots or trays in the frame, or plant directly in the soil on the floor of the frame. If you have a portable frame, move it to the garden in spring and fall to protect crops in place.

Plastic jugs can make handy individual plant protectors, but remove them on warm, sunny days to prevent overheating.

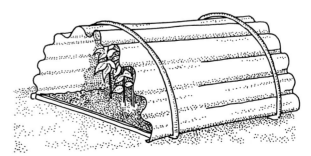

Make a rigid row cover with a length of translucent corrugated fiberglass, or buy a similar commercial product.

At season's end, dig up the remains of root crops like potatoes to prevent pests from overwintering on them.

Planting a cover crop is a great way to protect the soil from erosion or compaction over winter.

Putting the Garden to Bed

When all your plants are through producing for the season—except perhaps a few late crops snuggled in a cold frame or under row covers—it's time to clean up. Spring may inspire you to clean indoors, but fall is the best time to clean up out in the companion garden. Pests and diseases often linger on old plant debris or dig in near plant roots to spend the winter close to their preferred food source. When the plants go dormant, pests are trapped there, so it's the perfect opportunity for you to destroy them as you tidy up. If you get rid of old debris and weeds now, you will eliminate many pest and disease problems for the following growing season.

Dispose of Debris

Cut off old stems and put any that are disease- and seed-free in your compost pile. (Bury the rest or dispose of them with household trash.) You want to

If it's too late in fall to plant a cover crop, protect the soil with mulch.

Seek Out Stubborn Pests

If you have a particular pest problem that companion planting just won't control, find out where that insect—or its larval or pupal stage—hides during winter. Make a special effort to do away with it there before it returns for another season in your garden. Here are the hiding places favored by some troublesome garden pests:

- Squash vine borers hibernate about 1 inch (2.5 cm) below the soil surface.
- European corn borer larvae hide in old corn stalks and plant residue.
- Spotted asparagus beetles hibernate in the soil, often near old asparagus stalks.
- Potato tuberworms overwinter in old pieces of potato left in the ground or in other vegetable remains.
- Pickleworms roll themselves up in leaves in the garden or in weeds.
- Striped cucumber beetles hide under plant litter in the garden or burrow into mats of grass.
- Codling moth larvae overwinter in cocoons on the underside of loose apple bark.

Hardy root crops like parsnips and carrots can stay in the ground all winter under a thick layer of mulch.

clear out all the brown vegetation, with a few exceptions. You can leave fallen asparagus stems (if they are not bothered by asparagus beetles) to act as a mulch. And spare the dried seed heads of companion coneflowers (*Rudbeckia* and *Echinacea* spp.)—they can look attractive in winter and provide seeds that lure colorful birds to your garden.

Blanket the Soil

As garden space becomes vacant in late summer and fall, turn the soil with a spade or rotary tiller to expose hibernating pests, larvae, or eggs near the soil surface. This also kills many weeds. But to be doubly thorough,

Let some flowers go to seed to provide food for birds.

pull out any roots of perennial weeds that you turn up—otherwise they could resprout. If there are several weeks before the first hard frost, plant a cover crop, such as clover or winter rye, to protect the soil from erosion and compaction. Work the crop into the soil about 2 weeks before planting the following spring.

If you are planting a late vegetable crop but still want a cover crop for winter, try interplanting them. Plant the vegetables as usual for fall, and let them grow for about a month, keeping the space between plants weed-free. Then broadcast the seed of the cover crop over the growing area. By the time your late vegetables are ready for harvest, the cover crop will be large enough to walk on without damaging it.

A thick layer of mulch will provide ample protection for hardy root crops like parsnips, carrots, and beets that you leave in the ground. You also can mulch some perennials once the soil freezes in late fall. Mulch prevents the soil from heaving (shifting as it freezes and thaws), which can damage shallow-rooted perennials such as strawberries. Cover them with a loose, airy material such as straw or pine boughs.

Update Garden Records

When you are through outdoors, make some notes on the season's successes and failures. Write down which interplanting combinations worked well, what kinds of pests were around, and whether any companion plants deterred them. Note where you planted crops to control nematodes, chase away moles, or release allelopathic compounds for weed control. When you sit down to plan next year's garden, you'll have a good set of notes to guide your decisions. You can spend the winter anticipating an even better garden next year!

In cold climates, protect perennial plants over winter with a layer of mulch applied after the soil has frozen.

PLANT BY PLANT GUIDE

In a natural environment, plants live in balance with the insects, animals, and diseases around them. If the population of some pest increases dramatically, that insect's predators will increase as well. The predators may not increase fast enough to prevent serious plant damage, but the affected plants will eventually either recover or die to make room for new plants. In the grand scheme of things, the loss of an individual plant is of little consequence.

In your garden, though, you can't always afford to just let pests have free rein. The loss of one or two plants can spell the difference between a great harvest and no harvest at all. Your garden (even if it *is* organic) is an artificial environment, so you'll have to lend a hand to develop a balance between pests and plants. And that's what companion planting is all about.

One of the challenges of companion planting is finding the plant combinations that work best for you. Some combinations have been proven by research to work in certain situations. Others are based more on folklore and haven't been proven by facts. Both kinds of information can be helpful when you're looking for ideas of possible combinations. And this is what you'll find in this "Plant by Plant Guide."

When you sit down to plan your garden, make a list of the crops you want to grow. Then look up each one in this alphabetical guide to learn about its possible plant friends and enemies.

"Allies" offers specific suggestions for plant combinations that are supposed to enhance growth, flavor, and yield and those that are reputed to deter pests. Scientific confirmation is noted where published studies exist. Keep in mind that much more research is done on field crops than on the home garden crops; in many cases, no research studies have been conducted on the claims of companion gardeners.

"Companions" includes planting suggestions for each plant, based on its growth habit or ornamental attributes.

"Enemies" lists any plants that negatively affect growth. In some cases, you'll learn that the crop will harm the growth of other plants. Or you may find out about other plants that will interfere with the crop you want to grow.

"Growing Guidelines" supplies basic cultural information for each crop—from sowing times to spacing and harvesting tips. Each entry also highlights any special needs or procedures (like blanching or pest control) that the crop may need.

Last, the "Comments" section is a hodgepodge of fun information about the crop. You may learn about its history, uses, or garden habits.

Use the suggestions in this guide as a starting place for planning your companion garden. As you gain confidence in the method, conduct your own experiments, and keep track of the results over a period of years. Eventually, you will develop a valuable source of companion planting lore that is customized for your personal gardening conditions.

Over the years, many aspects of companion planting have been verified by scientific research; other companion recommendations have yet to be proven. Experiment to see which combinations work best for you.

| *Amaranthus* spp. | Amaranthaceae | *Angelica archangelica* | Umbelliferae |

AMARANTH

ANGELICA

Some companion gardeners believe amaranth benefits potatoes, onions, and corn planted nearby by bringing up nutrients from the subsoil with its deep taproot.

ALLIES: Spiny amaranth (*Amaranthus spinosus*) serves as a decoy crop for black cutworms; if this weed grows in your area, try leaving a few plants among your cucumbers, beans, or tomatoes.

COMPANIONS: Grow vegetable or grain amaranth among annual vegetables, or let a few plants stand in the strawberry bed. Ornamental species, such as love-lies-bleeding (*A. caudatus*) and Joseph's-coat (*A. tricolor*), have unusual flowers and colorful foliage.

ENEMIES: Field trials indicate that decaying plants may be allelopathic; soybean yields were reduced in one study.

GROWING GUIDELINES: Plant amaranth in fertile soil in full sun. Sow vegetable species in pots about 4 weeks before the last spring frost date. Transplant to the garden after second set of true leaves appear, spacing 6–12 inches (15–30 cm) apart. Or direct-sow after the last frost, when the soil is warm. Once plants are established (2–3 weeks after transplanting or 8–10 weeks after sowing), harvest tender young leaves weekly. Sow grain species in rows after danger of frost has passed. Thin to stand 8–10 inches (20–25 cm) apart. Hang mature seed heads to dry in a cloth sack. Beat the bag to thresh, and sift out the tiny, round seeds.

COMMENTS: Eat the young leaves in salad or cook like spinach. Grind seeds into flour or use whole.

Tall-growing angelica forms a striking clump of broad, lobed leaves. The sweetly scented, greenish flowers bloom in midsummer, attracting beneficial insects to your garden.

ALLIES: According to companion gardening lore, the pungent aroma of the angelica plant may help ward off aphids from nearby plants. Its airy white flower clusters attract parasitic wasps, lady beetles, lacewings, and other beneficial insects.

COMPANIONS: Plant angelica where its 5–8-foot (1.5–2.4 m) stems won't shade out lower-growing plants. It's a striking plant for flower borders or herb gardens, and it provides effective shade for summer lettuces.

ENEMIES: May have a negative effect on carrots.

GROWING GUIDELINES: Has a reputation for being temperamental about germinating. Grow from fresh seed; store seed in an air-tight container in the refrigerator until ready to plant. Sow in a partially shaded seedbed in late summer; do not cover. Thin to 1½ feet (45 cm) apart. Transplant to the garden the next year, spacing 3 feet (90 cm) apart in partial shade.

COMMENTS: The plant dies after flowering in its second or third year. Cutting off the flower stalks as they form will help prolong the life of the plant, but then you won't get the benefit of the flowers. To have a continuous crop, set out plants for the first few seasons; then let plants self-sow.

| *Pimpinella anisum* | Umbelliferae | *Malus pumila* | Rosaceae |

ANISE

Like other plants of the carrot family, anise produces lacy umbels of summer flowers that attract parasitic wasps and other beneficial insects to your garden.

ALLIES: Some companion gardeners say that a planting of anise will encourage coriander to germinate better and grow more vigorously. The strong smell of anise may repel aphids and fleas.

COMPANIONS: Set off this airy 2-foot (60 cm) tall plant with a planting of creeping thyme at its feet.

ENEMIES: May be detrimental to carrots.

GROWING GUIDELINES: Thrives in poor, well-drained soil in full sun and tolerates drought. Sow seed where it is to grow and thin to 1 foot (30 cm) apart. The plant may reach 2 feet (60 cm) high, but it tends to sprawl. Clip off seed heads into a bag before the seedpods shatter, but leave a few on the plant so it will self-sow for next year. Spread the seeds to dry on a piece of cloth in the sun. Store in sealed containers.

COMMENTS: Licorice-flavored anise seeds are used to flavor candy, pastry, cheese, and cookies such as biscotti—hard, half-round cookies that are favorites for dunking in coffee. An infusion of vermouth and anise flowers is used to flavor muscatel wine. Foxhounds are often trained to follow the scent of a sack scented with aromatic anise oil, and the mechanical hare at a greyhound track also carries this aroma to the trailing pack.

APPLE

Avoid planting a young apple tree in an old tree's "grave," as pathogens may linger in the soil. Remove dropped leaves and fruit to minimize the spread of diseases.

ALLIES: Research shows that carrot-family plants such as dill and Queen-Anne's-lace, with their abundant heads of flowers, attract parasitic insects that help control codling moths and tent caterpillars. Trap crops or repellents planted around or beneath apple trees are homegrown remedies that may help other problems; try mulleins (*Verbascum* spp.) to trap stinkbugs and nasturtiums to trap aphids.

COMPANIONS: Grow white clover, buckwheat, or fava beans as a groundcover beneath older trees to attract predatory insects such as ground beetles.

ENEMIES: Studies have found that ripe apples inhibit the development of potato plants. And some gardeners claim that potatoes interfere with photosynthesis and nitrogen absorption in apple trees.

GROWING GUIDELINES: Plant dormant young trees in early spring (or in late fall in Zones 8–10). Most cultivars require a second tree for pollination. Plant standard types 25 feet (7.5 m) apart; semidwarfs, 15 feet (4.5 m) apart; and dwarfs 10–15 feet (3–4.5 m) apart. Prune yearly in late winter or early spring to promote good air circulation.

COMMENTS: Choose resistant cultivars to minimize disease problems. A mulch of marigold roots was found to suppress populations of parasitic nematodes in the soil, leading to better growth of apple seedlings in infested soil.

Prunus armeniaca   Rosaceae

APRICOT

Some apricot cultivars need a second tree for pollination; others are self-pollinating. To get a good crop, make sure you know which kind you're buying!

ALLIES: Plant dill, parsnips, anise, and other carrot-family plants near your apricot tree; their flowers will attract beneficial insects that prey on codling moth larvae and tent caterpillars.

COMPANIONS: Underplant with a groundcover of white clover, buckwheat, or fava beans to attract predatory insects such as ground beetles.

ENEMIES: Apricots are susceptible to a virus-like disease called "yellows" and to fungal Verticillium wilt, which can be carried by nearby plants. Avoid planting apricots near plum trees or solanaceous plants such as tomatoes, potatoes, and eggplants.

GROWING GUIDELINES: Plant dormant trees in spring, spacing them 20 feet (6 m) apart. Apply a 2-inch (5 cm) layer of compost around the tree, keeping it 1 foot (30 cm) away from the trunk, to supply nutrients, conserve moisture, and prevent competition by weeds. Trees bear fruit in 4–5 years. Apricot blossoms are often damaged by late-spring frosts; avoid planting trees in an area where cold air collects, such as at the bottom of a hill. To prevent mold problems, thin out fruit so that it doesn't touch.

COMMENTS: Apricots fall victim to many of the same pests and diseases as peaches. Select cultivars that have been bred for disease resistance. If your summers are humid, look for cultivars such as 'Harglow', 'Hargrand', and others starting with "Har."

Asparagus officinalis   Liliaceae

ASPARAGUS

Wait to harvest your asparagus until the third spring after planting crowns or seedlings. Break spears off at soil level; using a knife can nick and damage the crown.

ALLIES: According to companion gardening lore, planting parsley or tomatoes with asparagus will invigorate both crops. Sprays or interplantings of parsley, tomatoes, and basil may discourage asparagus beetles (see "Herbal Sprays" on page 86 for directions on making sprays). Many companion gardeners find that asparagus grows well planted near basil.

COMPANIONS: Interplant early crops, such as lettuce, beets, or spinach, between the rows in spring. In Colonial times, grapes were sometimes trellised between the asparagus rows.

ENEMIES: None known.

GROWING GUIDELINES: Asparagus grows well in most areas that have either winter ground freezes or dry seasons. Choose a well-drained spot in full sun, and dig in plenty of compost or aged manure. It's important to prepare the soil well, since plants may stay in place for 20 years or more.

Most gardeners start asparagus from 1-year-old crowns. Buy all-male plants if available; females don't produce as many spears, but they can yield large numbers of seeds, which will lead to unwanted seedlings.

If you aren't in a hurry, it's also not difficult to grow asparagus from seed. In cold climates, sow seed indoors in peat pots in late February or early March; transplant the seedlings to a nursery bed after danger of frost has passed. In warm areas,

ASTERS

Ferny asparagus foliage can provide welcome shade for summer plantings of lettuce and spinach. Remove and destroy old foliage each spring to control pests and diseases.

Besides adding masses of welcome color, a border of perennial asters can attract a variety of beneficial insects to your late-season companion garden.

direct-sow into a nursery bed as soon as you can work the soil in spring. Sow two seeds at a time, 1 inch (2.5 cm) apart, in rows 1 1/2 feet (45 cm) apart. Germination can be slow, up to 30 days, although seed sown in warm areas may sprout in only 10 days. Thin the seedlings to stand 4 inches (10 cm) apart. Transplant them to their permanent bed at the end of summer.

Place transplants or purchased crowns 18–24 inches (45–60 cm) apart in a trench that is 12 inches (30 cm) wide and 8 inches (20 cm) deep. Allow 4–5 feet (1.2–1.5 m) between rows. Cover with 2 inches (5 cm) of soil. Add another 2 inches (5 cm) of soil every 2 weeks until the trench is filled. Mulch well and water regularly during the first 2 years after planting, and side-dress with compost or aged manure.

COMMENTS: Look for cultivars that are resistant to diseases like asparagus rust or Fusarium wilt. Handpick asparagus beetles that appear on spears or foliage. If diseases infect the bed, it's best to begin a new bed in another part of the garden.

Almost 100 years ago, two researchers discovered that a chemical compound in asparagus roots reduced populations of parasitic nematodes in soil. This line of research was apparently not pursued any further, but if you can spare some roots, chop them in the blender with water and use around tomatoes.

ALLIES: None known.

COMPANIONS: Perennial asters are useful for attracting beneficial insects such as hover flies and lacewings to the late-summer and fall garden. Branching species, such as the bushy aster (*Aster dumosus*), smooth aster (*A. laevis*), stiff aster (*A. linearifolius*), and calico aster (*A. lateriflorus*), are often home to praying mantids.

Asters complement many late-blooming plants in flower beds, borders, and naturalistic plantings. Try them with other beneficial-attracting flowers like perennial sunflowers (*Helianthus* spp.) and coneflowers (*Rudbeckia* spp.).

ENEMIES: None known.

GROWING GUIDELINES: Most asters prefer a sunny, well-drained site and thrive in average to lean soil. Many species are easy to grow from seed or divisions; propagate named cultivars by division in early spring or fall. New York aster (*A. novi-belgii*) and a few other species sometimes show signs of powdery mildew; give them a sunny, open site and thin crowded clumps to avoid problems.

COMMENTS: Grow several different species and cultivars to extend the color range and prolong the bloom season from midsummer through late fall.

Hordeum vulgare   Gramineae

BARLEY

Try barley as a cover crop to protect bare garden soil from erosion and weed invasion after you've harvested your early or midseason vegetable crops.

ALLIES: None known.

COMPANIONS: For a grain crop, replace early-maturing plots of lettuce and spinach or a cucumber patch that has lost its vigor with a late-season planting of barley. Alternate plots of corn or popcorn with plantings of beans, then replace harvested beans with a barley crop.

ENEMIES: In the first century A.D., Pliny observed in his *Natural History* that barley and a few other plants "scorch up" cropland. Extensive research on the effect of crop residues on lettuce seedlings appears to prove Pliny's case; barley residues were found to contain toxins that stunted the growth of nearby lettuce roots. While they are growing, barley plants exhibit an allelopathic action that reduces competition from neighboring weeds.

GROWING GUIDELINES: Plant in late summer or early fall for a thick cover crop. Prepare the seedbed in full sun in average, well-drained soil. Broadcast the seed by hand or with a crank-type seeder, using about 4 pounds per 1,000 square feet (1.8 kg per 93 sq m). Harvest the grain early in the following summer while the heads are still greenish. If a kernel dents with your fingernail but does not squash into milky mush, it's ready to harvest. Cut stems at the soil surface and hang in bundles to dry.

COMMENTS: Add barley to soups and other dishes, or use a blender to mill small amounts into flour.

Ocimum basilicum   Labiatae

BASIL, SWEET

Basil is a popular companion for tomatoes, both in the garden and the kitchen. It is sensitive to cold, so wait until the weather and soil are warm before planting outdoors.

ALLIES: Companion gardeners believe that basil improves the flavor and growth of tomatoes. Some are also convinced that basil or basil sprays protect tomatoes from insects and disease, although this remains unproven by scientific research. (See "Herbal Sprays" on page 86 for information on preparing sprays.)

COMPANIONS: Compact cultivars like 'Spicy Globe' make a neat edging along flower borders. Purple-leaved cultivars like 'Purple Ruffles' are great in flower beds as well as in vegetable gardens.

ENEMIES: Even in the 1600s, gardeners observed that rue and basil did not appear to be good neighbors. "Something is the matter," noted Nicholas Culpeper, in his *English Physitian and Complete Herball.* "This herb and rue will never grow together, no, nor near one another."

GROWING GUIDELINES: Sow seed $^1/_8$ inch (3 mm) deep in full sun, or set out transplants. Space plants 6–12 inches (15–30 cm) apart for small-leaved types such as 'Minimum'; allow up to $1^1/_2$ feet (45 cm) between plants for larger cultivars such as 'Genova'. Water and mulch to keep the soil evenly moist. Pinch or cut back flowering stems to keep the plant producing more leaves.

COMMENTS: Garden lore suggests that basil repels flies and mosquitoes: Try tucking a few stems into a bouquet on the patio table.

Phaseolus spp. and other genera   Leguminosae

Bean

Climbing beans are good companions for corn. The twining vines help to anchor the corn stalks against wind damage, and the roots add extra nitrogen to the soil.

To deter pesky Mexican bean beetles, some companion gardeners recommend planting aromatic herbs, such as winter or summer savory and rosemary, around your bean crops.

ALLIES: Companion gardeners maintain that interplanting tomatoes or corn with beans improves the growth and yields of both crops. Science documents a field study in which each tomato was surrounded by several bean plants, and both beans and tomatoes yielded top crops. Volatile compounds from soybeans and garbanzo beans have been shown to stimulate the uptake of phosphorus in corn plants.

Some companion gardeners recommend marigolds or potatoes with beans to repel Mexican bean beetles. Scientific studies with marigolds show reduced beetle populations, but a border planting of French marigolds (*Tagetes patula*) negatively affected the beans' growth. Interplanting potatoes with beans showed some success, though researchers suggested that it doesn't matter much what the interplanted crop is, as long as it doesn't host Mexican bean beetles.

To help repel black aphids from beans, try intercropping bush beans with garlic, or grow nasturtiums as a trap crop. Summer savory, which goes so well with cooked beans, is said to improve the growth and flavor of growing beans as well.

COMPANIONS: Celery, corn, and cucumbers are a few good companions for interplanting.

ENEMIES: Garden traditions are sometimes contradictory. While some companion gardeners recommend interplanting garlic with beans to repel insects, others say that any member of the onion family, including garlic, shallots, and chives, will be detrimental to growth and yield. Supposedly, beans also fail to do well when planted near sunflowers. American Indians, however, often surrounded their garden plots of corn, beans, and squash with an edging of sunflowers.

GROWING GUIDELINES: Sow seed in average to fertile, well-drained soil in full sun. Start planting around 2 weeks after the last spring frost date, when the soil is warm (seeds will rot in cold, wet soil). For an extended harvest, make successive plantings at 2–3-week intervals until 2 months before the average date of your first fall frost. Plant bush beans 1–1½ inches (2.5–3.75 cm) deep and 3–6 inches (7.5–15 cm) apart. For pole beans, set up vertical supports, like teepees or trellises, before you plant. Sow 2 inches (5 cm) deep and 10 inches (25 cm) apart. Pick green beans while young; pick fresh shell beans when plump but tender. Leave dry beans on the plants until they rattle in the pod.

COMMENTS: A mustard oil in the roots of turnips and parsnips was shown to have an insecticidal effect on Mexican bean beetles. You may want to mix the roots with water in a blender and use as a spray on bean plants.

Beta vulgaris   Chenopodiaceae

BEET

Companion planting lore holds that beets thrive when planted with onions or cabbage and its relatives. Harvest beet roots when small; pick tender leaves for cooked greens.

ALLIES: Try sprays or companion plantings of mints (*Mentha* spp.) or catnip (*Nepeta cataria*) to ward off flea beetles. (See "Herbal Sprays" on page 86 for directions on making sprays.)

COMPANIONS: Plant in alternate rows with other crops, even those that grow tall. (Although beets prefer full sun, they also tolerate partial shade.) Alternate beets in a row with onions or kohlrabi. Beets have attractive red-veined leaves that also make a nice addition to ornamental plantings.

ENEMIES: Some companion gardeners believe that beets do poorly when planted near pole beans or field mustard.

GROWING GUIDELINES: For best root development, beets need a sunny site with loose, fertile, well-drained soil that is free of rocks and stones. Sow seed 1 inch (2.5 cm) deep and 2 inches apart about a month before the last spring frost. Seedlings often come up in clumps; thin to stand 2 inches (5 cm) apart. Transplant thinnings to fill bare spots, or enjoy them in salads. Sow a fall crop in late summer.

COMMENTS: Leafminers and flea beetles are common pests, but usually cause only cosmetic damage and do not affect root yields. (If you are growing beets for their greens, floating row covers can help keep foliage pests away.)

Borago officinalis   Boraginaceae

BORAGE

Borage bears delightful blue star-shaped flowers that make it a fine plant for ornamental plantings as well as the vegetable patch. It will also attract large numbers of honeybees.

ALLIES: Some companion gardeners believe that borage improves the flavor and stimulates the growth of strawberries and other crops. "Among strawberries here and there sow some Borage seed," wrote William Coles some 350 years ago, "and you shall find the strawberries fare much larger than their fellows." Others believe that borage strengthens the resistance of neighboring plants to disease and pests. Borage also has an unsubstantiated reputation for deterring cabbageworms; experiment by planting it near your cabbage-family crops.

COMPANIONS: A planting of tall, sprawling borage is appealing in a wildflower garden or with shorter cultivars of sunflowers. Orchards may benefit from a border of borage, which attracts pollinating honeybees.

ENEMIES: None known.

GROWING GUIDELINES: Sow seed $^{1}/_{2}$ inch (12 mm) deep in average, well-drained soil in full sun, after danger of heavy frost has passed. Thin or carefully transplant seedlings to stand 2 feet (60 cm) apart. Occasionally, borage acts as a biennial, not blooming until the following year. Once it blooms, it will self-sow freely.

COMMENTS: Borage in teas or salads is said to create a feeling of well being and joy. A pretty way to serve borage is to freeze a flower in an ice cube and drop in lemonade or other clear, light-colored drinks.

Rubus spp.   Rosaceae

BRAMBLES

Flowering plants that attract beneficial predatory and parasitic insects can help protect your brambles from pest damage. Minimize disease problems by selecting resistant cultivars.

ALLIES: Encourage beneficial insects by planting dill and other flowering carrot-family flowers nearby.

COMPANIONS: Grapes benefit from nearby plantings of blackberries; the brambles serve as host plants for a parasitic insect that preys on grape leafhoppers, a pest of the vines.

ENEMIES: Remove wild brambles within 500 feet (150 m) of your plants to prevent the spread of viruses.

GROWING GUIDELINES: Plant dormant brambles in spring in deep, loose, well-drained soil with a pH near 6.5. Incorporate organic matter before planting. Plant in full sun in the North and in partial midday shade in the South to prevent sunscald of fruit. Space raspberries 1–3 feet (30–90 cm) apart and blackberries 5–6 feet (1.5–1.8 m) apart. Space rows at least 6 feet (1.8 m) apart. Train plants to a trellis for easier picking. Mulch deeply to inhibit weeds. Mow fall-bearing raspberries low to the ground after leaves drop in fall. Snip off fruiting canes of summer bearers after harvesting; cut young nonbearing canes back to 4 feet (1.2 m). Encourage side shoots of black and purple raspberries by cutting the tip off each cane when it reaches 3–4 feet (90–120 cm) high; after harvest, cut off fruiting canes low to the ground. Treat blackberries the same as black raspberries.

COMMENTS: Control aphids, as they carry viruses between plants.

Brassica oleracea, Botrytis group   Cruciferae

BROCCOLI

Aromatic herbs, including chamomile, dill, peppermint, rosemary, and sage, are said to be beneficial to broccoli and its relatives by discouraging pests.

ALLIES: Many companion gardeners believe that beans, celery, potatoes, and onions improve broccoli's growth and flavor.

COMPANIONS: Broccoli needs lots of calcium, so plant it with low-calcium feeders like beets, nasturtiums, marigolds, or sage.

ENEMIES: Many companion gardeners believe that broccoli and other cabbage-family plants are negatively affected by tomatoes. In scientific studies, decomposing broccoli residues were found to have a toxic effect on lettuce seedlings. It's probably a good idea to remove and compost decaying broccoli plants instead of turning them under.

GROWING GUIDELINES: Sow seed indoors, 1/2 inch (12 mm) deep and 2 inches (5 cm) apart, about 2 months before the last spring frost date. Set out seedlings or nursery-grown transplants about a month before the last frost date. Give them a site with fertile, well-drained soil and full sun. Space the young plants 12–24 inches (30–60 cm) apart. Sow a fall crop directly in the garden in July through August. Harvest the terminal bud while the florets are tightly budded and green. Broccoli is a heavy feeder, so top-dress with compost or feed with fish emulsion every few weeks.

COMMENTS: Cover plants with floating row covers to deter many broccoli pests.

Brassica oleracea, Gemmifera group Cruciferae	*Brassica oleracea*, Capitata group Cruciferae

BRUSSELS SPROUTS

CABBAGE

Companion gardeners believe that nearby plantings of beans, celery, potatoes, and onions will improve the growth and yield of brussels sprouts.

ALLIES: Try strong-smelling herbs, such as hyssop, peppermint, sage, and wormwood, to discourage aphids and other insect pests. Some scientists believe a masking effect is at work in these types of plantings, in which the mustard-oil odor of the brussels sprouts plant is hidden by other strong smells.

COMPANIONS: Plant flowering herbs such as chamomile and carrot-family plants like dill nearby to help attract beneficial insects.

ENEMIES: Many companion gardeners believe that tomatoes planted nearby have a detrimental effect on brussels sprouts. But research with cabbage plants indicates that tomatoes may offer some protection from whiteflies and cabbage flea beetles.

GROWING GUIDELINES: Brussels sprouts grow best in cool weather and thrive in fertile, well-drained soil in full sun. Direct-sow seed or plant nursery-grown seedlings as early as you can work the soil in spring; or start seed indoors 8–10 weeks before the last spring frost date. Direct-sow a fall crop outdoors in July. Sow seed ½ inch (12 mm) deep and 2 inches (5 cm) apart. Thin or space plants to stand 2 feet (60 cm) apart. Stake plants in windy areas. Using a twisting motion, remove sprouts starting from the bottom of the stalk upward.

COMMENTS: Brussels sprouts develop a sweeter taste after a light touch of frost.

Traditional gardening lore says that cabbage grows better when planted with celery, onions, and potatoes, although no research has yet been done to prove or disprove the idea.

ALLIES: Aromatic plants, including marigolds, nasturtiums, pennyroyal, peppermint, sage, and thyme, are a favorite in garden lore for their reputed insect-repellent powers; except for marigolds, however, they have shown no significant effects in scientific trials with cabbage. In fact, nasturtiums have been shown to actually attract cabbage flea beetles. Studies have shown that while marigolds do reduce flea beetles, they also apparently cause an allelopathic reaction that inhibits the growth of the cabbage. In other studies, marigolds reduced the number of cabbageworms on the plants, but the caterpillars ate even more voraciously, causing an equal amount of damage as in plants without marigold companions. Again, the yield was reduced, possibly because of an allelopathic substance.

Interplanting tomato rows with cabbage rows provided some protection from whiteflies and cabbage flea beetles in one study; researchers theorized that the smell of the tomatoes hid the smell of the cabbage. Another study showed that an interplanting of clover provided shelter for pest-eating ground beetles. Clover, lettuce, and weeds also help protect from infestations by making the cabbage hard to find.

COMPANIONS: Try a border of kale around your cabbage patch to decoy insects away from the cabbage heads. Grow cabbage with plants that won't compete

Colorful red cabbage is attractive as well as flavorful. Regular green cabbage can also look quite interesting when planted with purple-leaved 'Dark Opal' basil.

Many companion gardeners recommend planting Chinese cabbage with strong-smelling herbs—like pennyroyal, peppermint, sage, thyme, and wormwood—to deter pests.

for calcium, like sage and thyme. Or, if you have rich, fertile soil, interplant with other cabbage-family crops, such as broccoli and brussels sprouts, which share cabbage's heavy feeding requirements.

ENEMIES: Companion gardeners disagree about strawberries and cabbage as companions; some say the relationship is beneficial while others say it affects cabbage negatively. Pliny recommends against planting cabbages near grapes; in *Natural History,* he states, "The vine [grape] also abhors cabbage and all sorts of garden vegetables...and these unless a long way off make it ailing and sickly."

GROWING GUIDELINES: Cabbage does best in cool weather. For the spring crop, sow seed indoors, ¹/₄ inch (6 mm) deep, 8–10 weeks before the last spring frost date, or buy nursery-grown seedlings. Transplant to fertile, well-drained soil in full sun as soon as the soil can be worked, spacing plants 12–18 inches (30–45 cm) apart. Harvest the heads when they are round and full. In long-season areas, you can plant a late crop in July.

COMMENTS: Control insect infestations with handpicking, or avoid most pest problems by protecting plants with floating row covers. Some studies indicate that spraying with a solution of southernwood (*Artemisia abrotanum*) and water may help inhibit infestation by imported cabbageworms (see "Herbal Sprays" on page 86 for directions).

ALLIES: Companion gardening lore suggests that Chinese cabbage, like other cabbage-family crops, thrives when planted with celery, onions, and potatoes. Try planting mustard as a trap crop to lure flea beetles away from Chinese cabbage.

COMPANIONS: Alternate with brussels sprouts in the row. The form of the tall-growing, bare-stalked sprouts complements the loose heads of the Chinese cabbage, allowing good air circulation around the plants. Or plant Chinese cabbage at the base of pea trellises, where it will get some shade and wind protection. Some companion gareners let spent Chinese cabbage plants stand as a trap crop for aphids; pull and destroy infested plants.

ENEMIES: None known.

GROWING GUIDELINES: Chinese cabbage is easy to grow from seed. In areas with cool summers, sow indoors about 6–8 weeks before the last spring frost date. Plant seed ¹/₄ inch (6 mm) deep in peat pots. In areas with hot summers, sow for a fall crop about 10 weeks before the average date of the first fall frost in your area. Sow or transplant into fertile, well-drained soil in full sun. Thin or space small types to stand 6 inches (15 cm) apart and larger types 12 inches (30 cm) apart.

COMMENTS: Chinese cabbage actually includes a number of types of leafy and head-forming cabbages, including bok choy and choy sum.

Calendula officinalis   Compositae

CALENDULA

Colorful calendula flowers attract beneficial insects, but the plant itself is often beset by aphids, whiteflies, and other pests. It may be useful as a trap crop.

ALLIES: Some companion gardeners believe a border or interplanting of calendula protects plants against asparagus beetles, tomato hornworms, and other insects; this may be due to a masking effect or a repellent created by the pungent scent of its foliage. It is reputed to repel dogs when planted around shrubs and trees.

COMPANIONS: The cheerful flowers of calendula are a great accent for herb gardens and flower borders. This compact annual fits in easily with vegetable garden plantings.

ENEMIES: None known.

GROWING GUIDELINES: Calendula is easy to grow. Scatter seed in early spring in average, well-drained soil in full sun. Cut plants back to 3 inches (7.5 cm) after the first flush of bloom for color until frost, or sow again for fall blooms. Calendulas thrive in cool weather and keep blooming through the first light frosts. Let a few seed heads stand for self-sown plants next spring.

COMMENTS: In olden days, gold-orange calendula petals were popular in cooking, and their inclusion in certain concoctions supposedly allowed the consumer to see fairies. On a more practical note, you can use the crushed, dried petals as a substitute for the coloring effect of saffron.

Carum carvi   Umbelliferae

CARAWAY

Caraway is susceptible to many of the same pests and diseases as carrots, so it may be best to keep these two crops on separate sides of the vegetable garden.

ALLIES: None known.

COMPANIONS: Caraway is a good companion to peas. It is slow to germinate, but if sown with fast-maturing peas, caraway seedlings will fill in after you harvest the peas. Caraway has a long taproot that helps loosen compacted soil and bring up nutrients from the subsoil. This carrot-family plant also bears lacy white heads of tiny flowers that attract a multitude of insects, including predatory wasps and other beneficials.

ENEMIES: Some companion gardeners have observed that caraway does not grow well next to fennel.

GROWING GUIDELINES: Caraway grows well in average, well-drained soil, in full sun to partial shade. Sow seed shallowly in the garden in early spring or fall. Plants may bloom either the first or second year. After flowering, be sure to snip seed heads before the seeds loosen and fall. Hang the seed heads to dry above a tray, so the seed can drop when ripe. Allow a few weeks for drying, then store the seed in tightly closed containers.

COMMENTS: Nutty caraway seeds, with an almost licorice-like tang, are a savory addition to breads and baked goods. Try a sprinkle in split-pea soup or sauerkraut.

Daucus carota var. *sativa*   Umbelliferae

CARROT

Sweet, crisp, colorful carrots are one of the most trouble-free garden crops. They come in a variety of shapes and sizes, all high in vitamin A.

Leave a few carrots—or a whole row—to overwinter in the garden. They'll flower the next spring, drawing many parasitic wasps and other beneficial insects to your garden.

ALLIES: Companion gardeners say that interplanted radishes, peas, or sage can improve the flavor of carrots. Some believe that onions, leeks, and rosemary, perhaps because of their strong scent, repel root maggot flies. Interplanting with onions may also help repel carrot rust flies, a problem in Northwest gardens.

COMPANIONS: These light feeders grow well in company with most other garden vegetables.

ENEMIES: Folklore suggests that dill and anise cause poor growth in carrots.

GROWING GUIDELINES: Plant in full sun in deep, loose soil free of rocks. If you have clayey or stony soil, choose a short-rooted, ball-type cultivar such as 'Kundulus', 'Orbit', or 'Little Finger', and remove rocks from the top 3–4 inches (7.5–10 cm) of soil.

Start sowing about 3 weeks before the average date of the last spring frost. Sow about six of the tiny seeds to each inch (2.5 cm), in rows 1 foot (30 cm) apart, and cover lightly with fine soil or a sprinkling of sand. Water gently with a fine mist to avoid washing out seeds. Carrots germinate in about 2–3 weeks. No matter how careful you are when sowing, the seedlings usually need a rigorous thinning. When tops reach 1–2 inches (2.5–5 cm), thin plants to stand 1 inch (2.5 cm) apart. Thin again to 4 inches (10 cm) apart in another 2 weeks, so that roots have plenty of room to grow. Make

successive sowings every 3 weeks through the season until 3 months before the first fall frost for a continuous crop of young, tender carrots.

Water the patch before harvesting to soften the soil, and pull by hand (not with a spade) to avoid damaging the roots. Keep a ready supply of carrots all winter long by layering the roots in moist sand in a box. Top with straw for insulation and to retain moisture, and store in a cool place.

COMMENTS: Carrots, like other members of their botanical family (Umbelliferae), carry lacy umbels of tiny flowers when they bloom. Most gardeners never see a carrot flower, though, because the plants are biennial, and the roots are harvested before the second year.

If nematodes are a problem in your patch, causing little knots along roots and a stunted crop, plant the bed with French marigolds (*Tagetes patula*) the year before sowing carrots.

Nepeta cataria   Labiatae

CATNIP

If you plant catnip in the vegetable garden, be prepared to pull out self-sown seedlings and creeping shoots to control its spread, or grow it in an unused area.

ALLIES: Companion gardeners note that planting catnip near susceptible plants such as eggplants and turnips appears to reduce infestations of flea beetles. A scientific researcher isolated a compound from catnip and tested the insect-repellent qualities of its vapors. Besides repelling flea beetles, the vapor also chased away spittlebugs, ants, Japanese beetles, weevils, and a dozen other species. Controlled field research yielded sometimes conflicting results; the rampantly spreading catnip often inhibited the growth of companion plants.

COMPANIONS: Try a mulch of catnip branches around plants to take advantage of insect-repellent qualities without the competition.

ENEMIES: None known.

GROWING GUIDELINES: Catnip seeds are tiny and hard to handle; you could try sowing them outdoors in early spring. For more reliable results, start with a small nursery-grown plant or a division from a friend. Space clumps 18 inches (45 cm) apart. Catnip does well in full sun or partial shade, in average, well-drained soil.

COMMENTS: Place fresh catnip on shelves to help repel ants. A spray of catnip and water was shown to deter Colorado potato beetles (see "Herbal Sprays" on page 86 for directions). Cats will ignore catnip unless the leaves are crushed. Keep Kitty content all winter by cutting stems to dry in late summer.

Brassica oleracea, Botrytis group   Cruciferae

CAULIFLOWER

According to companion gardeners, the growth and flavor of cauliflower is improved by the presence of beans, celery, celeriac, onions, or potatoes growing nearby.

ALLIES: Aromatic plants, including pennyroyal, peppermint, sage, southernwood, and thyme, are also said to have a beneficial effect. Some companion gardeners believe that these plants, as well as tomatoes, may also repel pests. However, the mustard oil in cabbage-family crops is so pungent that not even powerfully scented herbs can disguise it entirely.

COMPANIONS: In rich soil, interplant cauliflower within the row with other plants of the cabbage family, such as broccoli and brussels sprouts. In average soil, plant cauliflower with light feeders like sage and thyme.

ENEMIES: Many companion gardeners believe that cauliflower inhibits the growth of grapes.

GROWING GUIDELINES: Start seed indoors in peat pots 4–6 weeks before the last spring frost, or buy nursery-grown seedlings in individual pots. Set out plants 18–24 inches (45–60 cm) apart in the garden. Sow a fall crop 2–3 months before the first expected frost. Water evenly and frequently, and use a thick mulch. To blanch, tie some leaves loosely over the top with rubber bands or twine when heads reach egg size. Heads are usually ready to pick after 5–7 days of blanching.

COMMENTS: Sprays of aromatic plants such as those listed above may have some effect as an insect deterrent (see "Herbal Sprays" on page 86 for directions). Or keep pests off plants with row covers.

Apium graveolens var. *rapaceum*   Umbelliferae

CELERIAC

Let a few celeriac plants stay in the garden to flower their second year. The blooms will attract beneficial insects, and you can save the seed for future planting.

<u>ALLIES</u>: Companion gardening lore recommends planting celeriac with beans, cauliflower, leeks, or tomatoes for healthy growth and good flavor.

<u>COMPANIONS</u>: Both leeks and celeriac are heavy potassium feeders; plant in alternate rows and feed with fish emulsion. Or try growing celeriac at the foot of trellised scarlet runner beans. A planting of winter vetch the year before enriches the garden bed for celeriac.

<u>ENEMIES</u>: None known.

<u>GROWING GUIDELINES</u>: Celeriac is a cold-tolerant plant that grows well in cool weather and can be overwintered with a heavy mulch. Start seed indoors about 6 weeks before the average date of the last spring frost in your area. After danger of frost has passed, set out plants into fertile, well-drained soil in full sun. Space plants 12–15 inches (30–37.5 cm) apart. As the root begins to enlarge (around the end of the summer), pull off some of the coarse outer leaves to keep the top of the crown smooth. Harvest by pulling up the plant when roots reach about 4 inches (10 cm) wide.

<u>COMMENTS</u>: Peel the celery-flavored root and add it to soups and stews.

Apium graveolens var. *dulce*   Umbelliferae

CELERY

Celery likes cool weather, plenty of water, and rich soil in sun or light shade. This shallow-rooted crop combines well with deeper-rooted plants, like beans and squash.

<u>ALLIES</u>: According to companion gardeners, celery thrives with leeks, tomatoes, cauliflower, cabbage, and bush beans.

<u>COMPANIONS</u>: Interplant with leeks in trenches, and fill gradually with soil to blanch both vegetables. Both are potassium-lovers; feed with fish emulsion to encourage better growth.

<u>ENEMIES</u>: None known.

<u>GROWING GUIDELINES</u>: Celery likes cool weather, plenty of water, and rich soil in sun or light shade. It needs a medium-long growing season to mature, but even young plants are flavorful and worth growing. Sow seed shallowly indoors about 8 weeks before the last spring frost. Set plants out when they are 6 inches (15 cm) tall, spacing them 6 inches (15 cm) apart. Water frequently to keep the soil evenly moist. Cut off stems as needed, or blanch the plant for a milder, less-bitter taste. Blanching also protects the stems from frost. To blanch, mound soil around the stems as they grow. When the stems are thick, tie the tops together and pop a coffee can or other light-excluding device over the plant for 2 weeks. Uncover and harvest by cutting off the plant above root level.

<u>COMMENTS</u>: If a tree casts its shadow on your garden, pick that corner for a celery crop. Stems will be looser and more strongly flavored than those of plants grown in sun.

Chamaemelum nobile   Compositae   *Anthriscus cerefolium*   Umbelliferae

CHAMOMILE, ROMAN   # CHERVIL

Fresh white daisies and ferny, low-growing foliage with the fresh smell of apple make chamomile a favorite with companion gardeners. The blooms also attract many beneficial insects.

Chervil bears heads of tiny white flowers that attract beneficial insect predators and parasites to the garden. Grow it as a border or interplant it with your vegetables.

ALLIES: Chamomile is reputed by companion gardeners to improve the flavor and growth of cabbages, onions, and aromatic herbs, although no scientific research has been done to confirm this. Its daisy-like flowers attract many insects, including beneficial hover flies and wasps.

COMPANIONS: This perennial herb spreads fast by rooting along the sprawling stems. Use it as a border for herb and ornamental gardens or as an edging for vegetable gardens. Try a chamomile lawn around a garden bench, where foot traffic is light.

ENEMIES: None known.

GROWING GUIDELINES: Start Roman chamomile from cuttings or divisions. Grow in light, well-drained soil in full sun to partial shade. Set plants 6 inches (15 cm) apart. Shear young plants by hand once or twice to encourage branching. If you're growing a chamomile lawn, trim established plants with a mower at a high setting to keep them bushy.

COMMENTS: Roman chamomile is a low-growing perennial. German chamomile (*Matricaria recutita*) has similar flowers but grows taller and is an annual. Roman chamomile is reputed to control damping-off disease when used as a spray (see "Herbal Sprays" on page 86 for directions). The fresh apple scent is welcome in tea and refreshing in a bath. Steep a large handful in a quart (1 l) of water for about 10 minutes, then strain off the scented water into the tub.

ALLIES: Some companion gardeners recommend planting chervil with radishes to improve their flavor.

COMPANIONS: Chervil grows well below taller plants that offer some shade.

ENEMIES: None known.

GROWING GUIDELINES: Sow seed in average, well-drained soil in full sun; do not cover. Keep the seedbed moist until the seeds germinate. Thin seedlings to 10 inches (25 cm) apart. Harvest leaves after about 6 weeks. Sow at 2-week intervals for a continuous crop. Leave seed heads on the plants to self-sow, or sow collected seed in fall for a spring crop.

COMMENTS: The warm pungency of chervil—like a combination of anise and parsley—is good in soups and other dishes. The leaves are often included with parsley, thyme, and tarragon in the *fines herbes* of French cooking. The plant has been used in folk medicine to treat gout, epilepsy, pleurisy, and high blood pressure, although none of these claims is supported by scientific evidence.

Allium schoenoprasum   Amaryllidaceae

CHIVES

Easy-to-grow chives add pretty pink or purple blossoms to the garden and a mild onion tang to soups, salads, and potato dishes. Pinch off spent flowers to prevent self-sowing.

<u>ALLIES</u>: Companion gardeners recommend chives to improve growth and flavor of carrots, grapes, roses, and tomatoes. Some suggest that a ring of chives around an apple tree may inhibit the growth of apple scab (possibly by affecting the spores carried on dropped leaves); others say chives ward off Japanese beetles or black spot in roses. No scientific studies have been conducted to confirm these reports.

<u>COMPANIONS</u>: Chives are too pretty to keep in the vegetable garden alone. Use them for a neat and attractive border planting, punctuate the corners or centers of herb beds with their spiky form, or weave a few clumps into the perennial border.

<u>ENEMIES</u>: Some companion gardeners believe that chives inhibit the growth of beans or peas.

<u>GROWING GUIDELINES</u>: Seeds require darkness to germinate. Sow a generous amount of seeds in each peat pot indoors. Cover the tray of pots with a piece of newspaper or cardboard, then be patient—they are slow to sprout. Transplant the young clumps, pot and all, to a sunny spot in average, well-drained soil. Space clumps 18 inches (45 cm) apart. Snip leaves when they reach 6 inches (15 cm) tall.

<u>COMMENTS</u>: Some companion gardeners recommend a spray of chives processed with water in a blender to deter mildew on cucurbits and gooseberries or black spot on roses. Snip fresh leaves into pieces and freeze in zippered plastic bags.

Chrysanthemum spp.   Compositae

CHRYSANTHEMUM

Unless you're growing them as a companion for tomatoes, keep chrysanthemums in the flower garden; they combine well with many late-blooming plants.

<u>ALLIES</u>: Research indicates that chrysanthemums may reduce nematode populations, especially when grown with tomatoes.

<u>COMPANIONS</u>: Several species of chrysanthemums, including *C. cinerariifolium* and *C. coccineum,* are a source of pyrethrum, a natural insecticide. Home-made sprays and dusts made of dried, ground flowers are effective against many insects, including beneficials. Apply them only when infestations of pests are uncontrollable by other means.

<u>ENEMIES</u>: In one study of the garden mum (*C.* x *morifolium*), a toxin was leached from the leaves by rainwater. The compound completely prevented lettuce seeds from germinating in one study and made the bed so inhospitable that not even the same species of mum could be successfully grown for several years.

<u>GROWING GUIDELINES</u>: There are over 100 species of mums, including annuals and perennials. All bear plentiful daisy-like flowers, though sizes, shapes, and colors of the blossoms vary widely. Plant or divide perennial types, like garden mums and Shasta daisies, in spring or early fall, in full sun and fertile, well-drained soil.

<u>COMMENTS</u>: Showy perennial garden mums are ideal companions to other late bloomers, such as fall asters (*Aster* spp.), 'Autumn Joy' sedum, and hardy ageratum (*Eupatorium coelestinum*).

Citrus spp.   Rutaceae   *Trifolium* and *Melilotus* spp.   Leguminosae

CITRUS   CLOVER

Plant a cover crop or allow some weeds to grow around your citrus trees to encourage predators and parasites of aphids, California red scale, and other troublesome pests.

Grow clover as a living mulch or a green manure crop. The flowers attract beneficial insects, and the nitrogen-fixing bacteria on the roots work to enhance soil fertility.

ALLIES: Companion gardeners and farmers in tropical climates suggest that citrus trees grow better with guava, live oak (*Quercus virginiana*), or rubber trees. Others recommend interplanting with coffee or pepper plants.

COMPANIONS: Plant a cover crop or allow some weediness around trees to encourage parasites of California red scale. Dill, caraway, and other plants with heads of many small flowers may also be useful to attract predatory insects.

ENEMIES: None known.

GROWING GUIDELINES: Buy lemons, oranges, and other citrus trees from local nurseries, which usually stock plants that are well suited to the area. Gardeners in cold climates can plant dwarf species in tubs, bringing them indoors for winter. Choose a sturdy tree with vigorous growth and no visible damage. Plant in full sun, with the graft union well above ground. Never let citrus trees dry out. Keep a close eye on plants in containers, making sure the planting mix stays moist. Avoid planting a new tree where an old one died; pathogens or allelopathic compounds may linger in soil.

COMMENTS: Process citrus fruits in the blender to make a spray that may help deter fall armyworms and bollworms on other crops. In one study, pests that ate treated leaves failed to thrive.

ALLIES: None known.

COMPANIONS: Clover is a good cover crop in orchards because it shelters predator beetles and attracts honeybees for pollination of the fruit blossoms. In vegetable gardens, sow white clover (*Trifolium repens*) between the rows or under plants as a living mulch, to control weeds and help conserve nutrients.

ENEMIES: Clover may be its own worst enemy. As early as 1804, farmers pointed to "clover sickness," a condition in which red clover (*T. pratense*), planted year after year in the same field, eventually fails. Toxins released by the roots account for the sickness, say research scientists. Decomposing plants may also affect the growth of wheat.

GROWING GUIDELINES: If planting clover for a living mulch, give the vegetable crop several weeks to get established before sowing the clover. For a mulch or cover crop, broadcast the seed by hand or use a crank-type spreader. Sow white clover at 4–8 ounces per 1,000 square feet (120–240 g per 93 sq m); white sweet clover (*Melilotus alba*) at 8–16 ounces per 1,000 square feet (240–480 g per 93 sq m); or yellow sweet clover (*M. officinalis*) at 8–16 ounces per 1,000 square feet (240–480 g per 93 sq m). Keep the seedbed evenly moist to promote good germination.

COMMENTS: Clovers are also great as green manures, especially before heavy feeders like corn.

Brassica oleracea, Acephala group   Cruciferae

COLLARDS

Collards adapt equally well to both hot- and cool-climate gardens. Keep the leaves damage-free with row covers, or try tomatoes or marigolds as companions to repel pests.

ALLIES: Planting tomatoes with collards has been shown in research to reduce flea beetles and diamondback moths. Marigolds may offer some protection against flea beetles and cabbageworms, but the marigolds may also reduce collard yields due to an allelopathic effect.

COMPANIONS: Companion gardeners sometimes recommend collards for a trap crop around the cabbage patch. However, research indicates that such a practice may only make things worse, increasing rather than decreasing the number of pests on the cabbages.

ENEMIES: Companion gardening lore warns against planting collards or other cabbage-family crops near grapes.

GROWING GUIDELINES: Sow early, about 4 weeks before the last spring frost. Broadcast seed or plant in rows, $^1/_4$ inch (5 mm) deep, in fertile, well-drained soil in full sun. Thin to 1 foot (30 cm) apart. Sow for a fall crop 8 weeks before the first frost. Harvest several leaves at a time, but save the center shoot so that it keeps producing new leaves.

COMMENTS: As with the other cabbage-family members, the flavor of collards sweetens after a few light frosts. Mulch the bed or row with deep, loosely piled leaves, so your collards will keep producing long after the rest of the garden succumbs to cold weather.

Coreopsis spp.   Compositae

COREOPSIS

The free-blooming golden yellow flowers of coreopsis bring butterflies and beneficial insects to the garden all summer long. Plant a border or row of them with your vegetables.

ALLIES: None known.

COMPANIONS: The abundant daisy-like blooms attract nectar- and pollen-seeking insects, including honeybees and beneficials.

ENEMIES: None known.

GROWING GUIDELINES: It's easy to grow most coreopsis species from seed sown indoors or outdoors; in fact, many readily self-sow. Propagate cultivars, such as the popular 'Moonbeam', by taking stem cuttings in early summer or dividing plants in spring or fall. Plant in average, well-drained soil in full sun. All species thrive in less-than-fertile soil; most are at home in very lean conditions.

COMMENTS: These native American wildflowers make superb garden flowers. Perennials and annuals alike bloom over a long period of time and rebloom if you remove the spent flowers. Thread-leaved coreopsis (*C. verticillata*) does well under dry conditions. Calliopsis (*C. tinctoria*) is a perky annual species available in tall or dwarf types, with masses of small gold daisies marked by a russet central blotch. It's effective in naturalized plantings or with ornamental grasses.

CORIANDER

CORN

Coriander's plentiful blooms attract beneficial insects to the garden, especially parasitic wasps. The pungent smell of its foliage may deter aphids from nearby crops.

Corn has a long history of companion planting lore. American Indian gardeners intercropped corn with beans and squash, a combination known as the "three sisters."

ALLIES: Coriander is reputed to help the germination and growth of anise. The pungent smell of its foliage may help deter aphids from nearby crops.

COMPANIONS: Interplant coriander anywhere in the garden. Its abundant blossoms increase the population of visiting beneficial insects. Coriander makes a good companion for biennial caraway because of their complementary growth habits.

ENEMIES: Some companion gardeners think that coriander inhibits seed formation in fennel.

GROWING GUIDELINES: Sow seed for this annual herb in average to lean soil in full sun where it is to grow; like most other carrot-family plants, it does not transplant well because of its taproot. Sow ¹/₂ inch (12 mm) deep and thin to 6 inches (15 cm) apart. Be stingy with fertilizer to keep flavor strong. Snip off small young leaves for use in salsas and Mexican or Middle Eastern dishes. Wait to harvest seed until the foliage and flower heads turn brown, but watch plants closely to catch the seed before it drops. Plants may self-sow if you let a few seed heads remain.

COMMENTS: The odor of the seed changes from mildly unpleasant to deliciously savory as it dries. Try ¹/₂ teaspoon of ground seed in banana or carrot bread for an unusual citrusy tang. Coriander root is popular in Thai cuisine.

ALLIES: The benefit of planting corn with beans has been upheld by scientific research, which showed increased yields when corn was grown with a legume. One study points out that an interplanting of soybeans encourages parasitic Trichogramma wasps, which help control corn earworms. Soybeans or peanuts also increase populations of predatory insects, which help reduce the number of corn borers. Beans and corn are mutually beneficial: Beans help keep fall armyworms in check on corn, notes one study, while corn minimizes leafhoppers on bean plants. Alternate rows of corn and bush beans, two rows of corn to one of beans. Or plant pole beans to climb corn stalks.

COMPANIONS: Sunflower borders were a tradition in American Indian gardens. British research indicates that strips of sunflowers alternated with corn will increase yields and decrease infestations of fall armyworms. Squash and pumpkins do well in the shade of the corn rows.

ENEMIES: The weed quack grass (*Agropyron repens*) appears to make nitrogen and potassium unavailable to corn, even when the area is heavily fertilized. Leached toxins from wheat-straw mulch reduced corn yields in farm research by 44–94 percent.

GROWING GUIDELINES: Plan your rotations so that heavy-feeding corn follows a nitrogen-boosting crop of beans, alfalfa, or clover. Sow seed after all

COSMOS

Start checking your corn for ripeness about 3 weeks after the silks appear. Press a fingernail against one of the kernels; if the sap looks milky, it's time to harvest.

Colorful cosmos is an excellent plant for attracting birds, bees, and other beneficials to your vegetable garden. Goldfinches are particularly fond of the seeds.

danger of frost has passed and soil is warm. Plant in blocks to assure good pollination, interplanting with single rows of beans if desired.

Plant four seeds at a time: "One for the blackbird, one for the crow, and that leaves just two to grow," in the words of an old prairie homily. Sow seed 1 inch (2.5 cm) deep, and space the groups 12–15 inches (30–37.5 cm) apart, in rows or in hills of soil. Thin if the blackbird and crow don't hold up their end of the bargain. Side-dress with organic fertilizer when plants are 6 inches (15 cm) tall and again when they are knee-high.

COMMENTS: Research is contradictory regarding the timing of corn-bean companion plantings. The tribe of Buffalo Bird Woman, a Hidatsa from what is now North Dakota, planted corn in May "when the wild gooseberry bushes were almost in full leaf," followed by squash in early June, and beans "immediately after squash planting." The key is to give the corn a few weeks' head start, so it will get established before the beans start climbing.

ALLIES: None known.

COMPANIONS: The flat daisy-like flowers of cosmos make a good landing platform for honeybees and beneficial insects seeking nectar or pollen. Plant either *Cosmos bipinnatus*, the old-fashioned, ferny-foliaged plant with pink, red, and white flowers, or *C. sulphureus*, the hot-colored, shorter type. The abundant foliage offers shelter to predatory insects.

ENEMIES: None known.

GROWING GUIDELINES: Cosmos are easy to grow from seed and easy to transplant, even when quite large. After danger of frost has passed, direct-sow seed ¼ inch (6 mm) deep in average, well-drained soil in full sun. Thin seedlings to stand about 3 inches (7.5 cm) apart, and pinch them when young and single-stemmed to encourage bushiness and branching. *C. bipinnatus* grows fast and lush, and it occasionally falls over from its own weight, snapping a heavy branch of buds or bloom. To salvage the plant, stick the broken end of the branch into the ground a few inches deep, or lay it horizontally and mound 2–3 inches (5–7.5 cm) of soil over the stem. Keep the soil wet while new roots form from the stem. It will recover in less than a week.

COMMENTS: Both types of cosmos are beautiful in bouquets. Try a few stems of orange 'Klondike' blooms, buds, and spiky seed heads in a green vase for an arrangement of almost oriental simplicity.

CUCUMBER

Cucumbers are reputed to grow better when planted with beans, cabbage, corn, peas, or radishes. Lettuce, celery, and Chinese cabbage grow well in the shade of trellised cucumbers.

<u>ALLIES</u>: Some companion gardeners believe that radishes lure away cucumber beetles or that pungent-smelling marigolds repel them. Research has shown that cucumbers interplanted with broccoli or corn are less likely to be ravaged by cucumber beetles or affected by the bacterial wilt the beetles carry. Spiny amaranth (*Amaranthus spinosus*) plants standing among cucumbers will serve as a trap crop for black cutworms.

<u>COMPANIONS</u>: Try cucumbers with cabbage-family crops, such as cabbage, broccoli, and cauliflower; by the time the cucumbers begin to sprawl, the earlier crops should be ready for harvesting.

<u>ENEMIES</u>: Potatoes growing near cucumbers are reputed to be more susceptible to Phytophthora blight. Companion gardeners also warn that aromatic herbs and cucumbers do not make good neighbors.

<u>GROWING GUIDELINES</u>: Grow cucumbers in hills or rows in fertile, well-drained soil in full sun. Sow seed ½ inch deep, or set out transplants 3 weeks after the last spring frost date, when soil has warmed. Thin or space plants to stand 12 inches (30 cm) apart. Water regularly to keep the soil evenly moist and help prevent bitter fruit. Apply an organic fertilizer, like fish emulsion, monthly.

<u>COMMENTS</u>: If diseases are a problem in your area, select disease-resistant cultivars such as 'Marketmore 76' or 'Sweet Slice'.

DAHLIA

Dahlias are available in many colors and flower forms. The double-flowered types may be more decorative, but the daisy-like forms are more attractive to beneficials.

<u>ALLIES</u>: None known.

<u>COMPANIONS</u>: Dahlias may be worth a try as a trap crop for cucumber beetles and grasshoppers; the pests devour the flowers. Corn stem borers also attack dahlias. However, some gardeners feel that planting these colorful flowers in the vegetable garden will just attract more of these pests.

<u>ENEMIES</u>: None known.

<u>GROWING GUIDELINES</u>: Grow dahlias from seed, nursery-grown bedding packs, or tuberous roots. Wait until the ground has warmed and danger of frost is long past before planting out market packs or tubers. Plant in deep, fertile, well-drained but moisture-retentive soil enriched with organic matter. When plants reach 6 inches (15 cm) high, pinch out the center growing tip to encourage branching.

Part of the fun of growing dahlias is collecting the bounty of tubers at the end of the season. Cut back after foliage is killed by frost, then lift the clump. Store the root clumps in damp vermiculite in a cool place. In spring, separate the tubers so that each piece has at least one eye (bud) at the stem end, and replant. In Zones 8–11, dahlias are perennial and overwinter in the ground if soil is well drained and does not freeze.

<u>COMMENTS</u>: Try 'Redskin', available in a variety of blossom colors, all with showy red leaves.

DILL

Dill is a useful plant in the companion garden, thanks to its big, airy umbels of many tiny flowers. It may also be effective as a trap crop for thick, green tomato hornworms.

ALLIES: Mud daubers and other large predatory wasps, as well as many smaller beneficials, visit dill flowers regularly. Companion gardeners say that dill improves the growth and health of cabbage and related crops. It's also reputed to repel aphids and spider mites, most likely because of its aroma.

COMPANIONS: Sow dill with lettuce, onions, or cucumbers; the plants' habits complement each other well.

ENEMIES: Many growers are convinced that dill reduces the yield of carrots. This belief may be rooted in the fact that both plants are susceptible to some of the same diseases. Some companion gardeners believe that tomatoes planted near dill will fail to thrive.

GROWING GUIDELINES: Dill can be temperamental about germinating. It sprouts better in cool rather than hot weather. Sow seed ¹/₄ inch (6 mm) deep and 4 inches (10 cm) apart in spring in average, well-drained soil in full sun. Thin seedlings to stand 8–12 inches (20–30 cm) apart. Sow every 2 weeks for a continuous supply. Once you have a thriving dill patch, chances are you'll have it for years; it self-sows liberally.

COMMENTS: Don't be alarmed by an infestation of green-black-and-yellow caterpillars on your dill. Let the creatures feed; they'll turn into graceful black swallowtail butterflies.

EGGPLANT

Companion gardening lore suggests growing eggplants with beans, peppers, and tomatoes. The aromatic scent of tarragon and thyme are reputed to repel pesky flea beetles.

ALLIES: Green beans planted around eggplants may protect them from Colorado potato beetles, perhaps by making the fruits hard to find.

COMPANIONS: Use the space between eggplant seedlings to grow an early crop of lettuce. The attractive fruits and pretty star-shaped flowers of some eggplants, make them useful as ornamentals, too. Try one or three eggplants as the center of a bed, surrounded with kale and purple or green basil.

ENEMIES: None known.

GROWING GUIDELINES: Eggplant is a warm-weather crop that thrives in areas with long, hot summers. Start seed indoors 6–9 weeks before the average last frost date. Sow seed ¹/₄ inch deep and keep warm. Move 3-inch (7.5 cm) seedlings to individual pots. Transplant to the garden in full sun after the soil is well warmed, spacing plants 24–30 inches (60–75 cm) apart. Water liberally during the growing season. This heavy feeder benefits from monthly applications of an organic fertilizer, like fish emulsion. Handpick pests or protect plants from damage with floating row covers. Harvest fruit at any size while it is still glossy; frequent picking will keep the plant bearing.

COMMENTS: 'Black Beauty' is a classic, large, dark purple-skinned cultivar, but it takes nearly 2¹/₂ months to mature. For an earlier harvest, try 'Dusky' or 'Ichiban', with long cylindrical fruits.

EUCALYPTUS

FENNEL

In warm climates, eucalyptus trees grow outdoors and can be striking landscape plants. In cool climates (north of Zone 8), grow them in pots and bring them inside in winter.

ALLIES: None known.

COMPANIONS: The brushy flowers of eucalyptus are useful for attracting honeybees and yield tasty honey. Silver dollar gum (*Eucalyptus cinerea*) and lemon gum (*E. citriodora*) are two appealing species suited to container growing.

ENEMIES: Eucalyptus are detrimental to most neighboring plants due to allelopathic substances produced by their roots and vegetative parts. Research with cucumbers shows that the common blue gum (*E. globulus*) inhibits the growth of the vegetables as well as other plants.

GROWING GUIDELINES: Eucalyptus transplants easily, and most species grow rapidly from cuttings. Plants need full sun and well-drained soil. Prune as needed to keep plants in bounds.

COMMENTS: There are more than 500 species of eucalyptus; all are native to Australia. These trees are very efficient at scavenging water. This trait makes them well adapted for low-rainfall areas; unfortunately, it also makes it difficult to grow other plants around these water-hogging trees.

The natural oil, with its distinctive menthol-camphor smell, is effective in treating upper respiratory problems. Plants are rarely troubled by pests, and some companion gardeners say a spray made from eucalyptus foliage processed in a blender helps deter pests in the garden.

Most companion gardeners keep fennel away from the vegetable garden, alleging that this licorice-scented herb inhibits the growth of bush beans, kohlrabi, tomatoes, and other crops.

ALLIES: None known.

COMPANIONS: Plant fennel in an ornamental border rather than in or near a vegetable garden. Its lacy leaves and airy flower heads combine well with flowering ornamentals. Wasps and other beneficials are attracted by the flowers.

ENEMIES: Coriander planted nearby is reputed to prevent fennel from forming seeds.

GROWING GUIDELINES: Fennel is perennial in warm climates, although it is usually grown as an annual. Sow seed shallowly in spring in average, loose soil in full sun; plant seeds in fall for an early-spring crop. Keep the seedbed moist until sprouts appear. Thin seedlings to stand 6 inches (15 cm) apart. Snip leaves for the kitchen as soon as the plant is well established; chop and freeze them in zippered plastic bags for a ready supply. To collect the seed, snip ripe seed heads into a paper bag.

COMMENTS: The raw seeds were once considered to be an appetite suppressant; the seeds do make an agreeable snack to nibble on.

FEVERFEW

FLAX

Biennial or perennial feverfew is a favorite of companion gardeners for its reputed ability to repel aphids and root knot nematodes. It is also an attractive ornamental.

ALLIES: The daisy-like flowers, especially on single-flowered types, attract foraging beneficials, and the bushy foliage provides shelter to predatory insects. Some companion gardeners recommend feverfew to help repel root knot nematodes. If your garden soil is infested with these pests, try a companion planting of feverfew with susceptible crops such as tomatoes, peppers, and lettuce. Or apply a mulch of feverfew branches around these crops so that the plant toxins leach into the soil.

COMPANIONS: Interplant feverfew in the vegetable garden or grow it in ornamental plantings. Try a circle of it around roses for an attractive (and possibly pest-controlling) combination.

ENEMIES: Some companion gardeners say that bees hate the smell of feverfew and will not visit other flowers planted near it.

GROWING GUIDELINES: Sow seed shallowly outdoors after danger of frost has passed, or plant divisions. Feverfew thrives in average, well-drained soil in full sun; it will also grow in partial shade but develops a more open habit. Pinch young plants to encourage bushiness. Cut back after bloom for a second crop of flowers.

COMMENTS: Sprays and dusts made of the dried, ground flowers may be effective against many insects, but they can kill beneficials as well as pests; apply them only as a last resort.

Flax may be a friend to carrots and potatoes and a foe to potato beetles. The sky blue blooms are best appreciated by early risers; the flowers close up in the midday sun.

ALLIES: Companion gardening tradition recommends planting flax to improve the growth and flavor of carrots and potatoes. Flax may offer some protection against Colorado potato beetles, perhaps because of the tannin and linseed oil in the plant.

COMPANIONS: Think carefully before you decide to plant flax in the vegetable garden. Ancient lore holds that flax "scorches up" cropland, an observation that may indicate allelopathic reactions.

ENEMIES: In the nineteenth century, a Swiss botanist observed that spurge (*Euphorbia* spp.) and scabious (*Scabiosa* spp.) were detrimental to the growth of flax.

GROWING GUIDELINES: Annual flax grows readily from seed sown in spring. Thin plants to 4 inches (10 cm) apart in mass plantings. Start perennial species by sowing seed indoors or outside in a nursery bed in late summer or fall. Plant annual and perennial flax in full sun in light, well-drained, average to lean soil. Both types self-sow.

COMMENTS: Annual flax is a common escapee from American gardens and can sometimes be found growing "wild" in great stretches along roadsides. The seed is a favorite of seed-eating birds, including goldfinches, house finches, and purple finches. It often shows up in premium birdseed mixes and sprouts from spilled seed beneath feeders. Collect your own seed for winter feeding by shaking the seed heads into a paper bag.

Allium sativum   Amaryllidaceae

GARLIC

Garlic sprays may help repel or inhibit Japanese beetles, aphids, weevils, snails, spider mites, and other pests. Garlic's effectiveness as a companion has yet to be proven.

ALLIES: Garlic is often recommended by companion gardeners as an insect-repelling plant, especially for planting around roses and for deterring Japanese beetles and aphids. Science has proven the insecticidal qualities of garlic sprays, but its effectiveness as a companion plant in the garden is unconfirmed.

COMPANIONS: Plant garlic between tomatoes, eggplants, or cabbage plants, or use it as a border planting.

ENEMIES: Garlic, like onions, is said to have a negative effect on peas, beans, and other legumes.

GROWING GUIDELINES: Plant garlic in fall, around Columbus Day, for a vigorous crop. Garlic needs a chilling period for best growth, and fall-planted bulbs will benefit from the winter cold. The bulbs will put out a few roots before winter, but green shoots usually won't appear until spring.

Give garlic a site with loose, rich soil in full sun. Plant cloves 2 inches (5 cm) deep and 4 inches (10 cm) apart. Mulch to keep weeds down, and water during dry spells.

A 20-foot (6 m) row will yield 5–10 pounds (2.5–5 kg) of garlic. Timing the harvest is a little tricky: Too early and bulbs will be small; too late and the outer skin may tear, making the bulbs store poorly. Wait until leaves begin to turn brown, then check the status of one head before you harvest

Each garlic bulb contains many smaller cloves. Separate the cloves in fall and plant them individually; they'll mature into fat bulbs by the following summer.

the whole crop. Hang bulbs by the leaves to dry, or weave them into a braid.

COMMENTS: Even in the 1800s, companion gardeners recognized garlic as a repellent. *The New York Farmer and American Gardener's Magazine* noted that "Snails, worms, and the grubs or larvae of insects, as well as moles and other vermin, may be driven away by placing preparations of garlic in or near their haunts."

Garlic oil is a proven insecticide and may have some effect on fungal or bacterial diseases. Researchers in England reported kills of aphids and onion flies from an oil of garlic emulsion. Other researchers used a garlic-based oil to kill mosquitoes. Some scientists observed that timed-release garlic capsules kept deer away from orchard trees.

For an all-purpose insect spray, add 3 ounces (85 g) of finely chopped garlic cloves to 2 teaspoons of mineral oil. Soak 24 hours or more, then stir in 1 pint (600 ml) of water and strain out the garlic. Spray plants with a solution of 1 tablespoon of oil to 1 pint (600 ml) of water. Test the mixture on a few leaves to check for injury from the oil before spraying whole plants. If no damage is evident after 2–3 days, spray plants thoroughly. This preparation will kill beneficial insects as well as pests, so use it only as a last resort.

Pelargonium spp.   Geraniaceae

GERANIUM

The dense, leafy growth of geraniums provides welcome hiding places for insect predators—especially spiders. You will enjoy the colorful flowers and appealing fragrances.

ALLIES: The showy flowering types of geranium are reputed to repel cabbageworms, corn earworms, and Japanese beetles. The scented ones are thought to deter red spider mites and cotton aphids. Some companion gardeners believe that white-flowered geraniums are effective as a trap crop for Japanese beetles; handpick the beetles from the leaves.

COMPANIONS: Interplant flowering or scented geraniums with vegetables—especially among cabbage and its relatives—or use as a border to the vegetable garden. Plant geraniums around roses for a pretty (and possibly pest-controlling) combination.

ENEMIES: None known.

GROWING GUIDELINES: Geraniums are easy to start from cuttings; some types will also grow from seed. Grow plants in full sun in lean to average, well-drained soil. Remove spent flowers on seed-grown plants to encourage more blooms. In frost-free climates, geraniums are perennial; elsewhere, take cuttings in late summer or pot up plants when frost threatens and bring indoors to overwinter. Plants grow tall and crooked with age, an appealing look to some companion gardeners but not to others. To reclaim an old plant, cut the stems back to short stubs; this will encourage vigorous new growth.

COMMENTS: Keep a pot of scented geraniums near walkways, where passersby will brush against the foliage and release the fragrance.

Solidago spp.   Compositae

GOLDENROD

Goldenrod offers attractive shelter to praying mantids and other predatory insects; in winter, you'll often see foamy-looking, brown mantid egg cases on old stems.

ALLIES: Goldenrod is one of the best plants for attracting beneficials to the garden. Its fall-blooming plumes or spikes are tightly clustered with thousands of tiny flowers rich with pollen and nectar. Blue mud daubers, hornets, hover flies, and a myriad of other smaller predatory and parasitic beneficials come to take advantage of the feast.

COMPANIONS: Plant goldenrod in masses or weave clumps into ornamental plantings near the vegetable garden. Many species self-sow freely or spread quickly by creeping roots, so don't invite them into the vegetable patch. Plumes of goldenrod and purple asters are the perfect combination for fall, in fields or a flower border.

ENEMIES: Some research indicates that goldenrod may inhibit the germination and growth of sugar maple (*Acer saccharum*) and black locust (*Robinia pseudoacacia*) by releasing an allelopathic substance.

GROWING GUIDELINES: Most goldenrods thrive in full sun to partial shade in average soil; rich fertile soil promotes soft stems that are prone to flopping. Divide plants every few years in spring or after flowering.

COMMENTS: Goldenrods are often mistakenly blamed for causing drippy noses and watering eyes in fall. The real culprit is an inconspicuous weed called ragweed, which produces allergy-causing pollen grains.

Vitis spp. Vitaceae

GRAPE

For centuries, grape growers have recommended planting hyssop near the vines to increase yields. Cabbage and radishes growing nearby may have the opposite effect.

ALLIES: Companion gardeners note that legumes (like peas and beans) may benefit grapevines.

COMPANIONS: Grow grapes near blackberries, which serve as a host for parasites of grape leafhoppers; in studies, these parasites drastically reduced populations of the pest.

ENEMIES: Cabbage and radishes have long been thought to affect grapes negatively. Pliny the Younger pointed out some 2,000 years ago, "The nature of some plants though not actually deadly is injurious owing to its blend of scents or juice—for instance the radish and laurel are harmful to the vine...." Pliny also reported, "The vine also abhors cabbage and all sorts of garden vegetables, as well as hazel; and these unless a long way off make it ailing and sickly...."

GROWING GUIDELINES: Plant dormant vines in spring in loose, deep, fertile soil, liberally enriched with organic matter. Grapes thrive at a pH of 5.0–6.0 and need adequate amounts of nitrogen, magnesium, and potassium; test your soil before planting and correct any deficiencies. Cut back new vines to two live buds, and train shoots to a trellis as the vines grow. Mulch lightly with compost; too much fertilizer causes rampant growth of the vines and a smaller crop of fruit.

COMMENTS: Pruning in mid- to late-winter encourages optimum fruit production, but even a neglected vine may produce some luscious bunches.

Armoracia rusticana Cruciferae

HORSERADISH

Horseradish may be a good companion for potatoes, but be warned that it can spread rampantly. New plants will spring up from root pieces that break off during harvesting.

ALLIES: Some companion gardeners claim that horseradish repels blister beetles—a pest of potatoes—and recommend that the two be planted together. However, be warned that horseradish can spread fast in loose, fertile garden soil.

COMPANIONS: It's best to give horseradish a permanent spot of its own, where you can keep it under control. If you do want to grow it next to your potatoes, control its spread by planting it in a bottomless bucket that you've sunk in the soil.

ENEMIES: None known.

GROWING GUIDELINES: Buy plants, or plant a piece of root bought at the grocery store. Horseradish will root quickly from even a small-sized root cutting; plant it about 2 inches (5 cm) deep, small-end down, in moist, rich soil in full sun. Deep, loose, rock-free soil will encourage the longest, straightest roots. Keep well watered until leafy shoots appear. Water regularly in late summer when roots are fattening. Dig in October or November, before the ground freezes. The pieces you miss will renew the patch next spring.

COMMENTS: Some companion gardeners grind the roots for a spray for their fruit trees, claiming it has antifungal properties. Chop a bit of the leaf to add zing to salads. Peel and grate roots, and add vinegar or mayonnaise to make a tangy complement to beef, fish, potato salad, and other foods.

Hyssopus officinalis   Labiatae

HYSSOP

Hyssop is reputed to repel flea beetles, lure away cabbage moths, and otherwise deter pests from garden crops, probably because of its strong, camphor-like odor.

ALLIES: Long-standing tradition holds that a nearby planting of hyssop increases the yield of grapevines. It is also recommended for orchards because its flowers are a magnet for honeybees.

COMPANIONS: Plant hyssop around the feet of grapevines and between cabbages and its relatives (like broccoli and cauliflower). If you keep bees, plant hyssop near the hive; the collected nectar will flavor the honey. This perennial herb makes an attractive short evergreen hedge and is also good in ornamental beds.

ENEMIES: According to folklore, radishes planted near hyssop will not thrive.

GROWING GUIDELINES: Start from nursery-grown plants, or sow seed ¼ inch (6 mm) deep in early spring. Thin or space plants to 12 inches (30 cm) apart. Hyssop grows well in average, well-drained soil in full sun. Multiply your planting by rooting 6-inch (15 cm) stem cuttings or dividing clumps in spring or fall. The plants are perennial but become less vigorous after 5 years or so. Replace with new plants started from cuttings or division.

COMMENTS: This pretty blue-flowered plant is one of the better-behaved members of the mint family; it doesn't spread rampantly.

Brassica oleracea, Acephala group   Cruciferae

KALE

Like cabbage, broccoli, brussels sprouts, and other cabbage-family plants, kale is said to do well when planted with beans, potatoes, celery, and onions.

ALLIES: Some companion gardeners are convinced that aromatic herbs, such as dill, mint, sage, and rosemary, improve the flavor of kale and other cabbage-family members.

COMPANIONS: Plant with late cabbage or potatoes. Use ornamental types to accent flower or vegetable plantings.

ENEMIES: Many companion gardeners believe grapes fail to thrive when planted near kale; others volunteer strawberries and tomatoes as unsuitable companions.

GROWING GUIDELINES: Sow seed ½ inch (12 mm) deep in fertile, well-drained soil in full sun in early spring. Thin to 2 feet (60 cm) apart. Kale has few problems with pests and diseases, but it grows poorly when temperatures climb higher than 75°F (24°C). Harvest outer leaves for cooking and tender inner leaves for salads. The harvest lasts a few weeks, until leaves get tough and stringy. Sow a fall crop 6 weeks before the average date of the first fall frost.

COMMENTS: This cool-weather green has a mustardy bite. As with many cabbage-family crops, a light frost sweetens the flavor. Today, it's a good bet that more gardeners grow kale for ornament than for the table. Decorative cultivars such as 'Peacock Red' have frilled leaves and spectacular coloring that deepens in tone as cool weather advances.

Brassica oleracea, Gongylodes group   Cruciferae

KOHLRABI

Lavandula angustifolia   Labiatae

LAVENDER

Kohlrabi grows well with other cabbage-family plants in nutrient-rich soil. Harvest when the swollen stem base is about the size of a silver dollar for the best flavor.

ALLIES: Companion gardeners say that kohlrabi—like its relatives in the cabbage family—grows particularly well when planted near onions, beets, cucumbers, and aromatic plants such as dill, mint, and sage.

COMPANIONS: In fertile soil, interplant kohlrabi with other members of the cabbage family, such as broccoli, cabbage, and cauliflower, which share its heavy feeding habits.

ENEMIES: Companion gardening lore suggests that kohlrabi may fail to thrive when planted with strawberries, tomatoes, or pole beans.

GROWING GUIDELINES: Kohlrabi is a cool-weather crop. Plant in fertile, well-drained soil in full sun, sowing seed ¼ inch (5 mm) deep, as soon as the ground can be worked. Thin to 5 inches (12.5 cm) apart. Provide plenty of water, and harvest before hot weather sets in and increases the "heat" of the bulb. Sow a fall crop 10 weeks before the first fall frost. As with other cabbage-family vegetables, a light touch of frost enhances the flavor.

COMMENTS: Kohlrabi keeps for months when refrigerated in the vegetable-crisper drawer. Slice the bulbous, aboveground stem base thinly or julienned for salads. Boil or steam the whole bulbs for a vegetable dish with a taste somewhere between turnip and cabbage. Thin raw slices are a good low-calorie nibble; they have a delicious crunch like water chestnuts when steamed or lightly stir-fried.

Some companion gardeners claim that lavender acts as a fly and tick repellent. Old-time lore carries it a step further and recommends lavender for warding off evil spirits.

ALLIES: Lavender is useful in the garden because its plentiful flowers attract nectar-seeking insects, including beneficials.

COMPANIONS: Plant lavender as a hedge or border, or incorporate it into vegetable and ornamental gardens to increase populations of visiting beneficial insects.

ENEMIES: None known.

GROWING GUIDELINES: You can start lavender from seed, but germination is slow and seedlings may vary widely in plant habit and flowering qualities. Most nurseries start their plants from cuttings. Plant lavender in dry, light, gravelly or stony soil in full sun. Clip back periodically the first year to encourage a dense branching structure. Plants often weaken after 5 years; start new ones from cuttings taken in summer.

COMMENTS: Used in a spray, lavender is reputed to control pests of cotton (see "Herbal Sprays" on page 86 for directions). It has also shown some repellent effect toward clothes moths; dry a sprig and slip it in a pocket or pin it to a sleeve in sweater drawers or closets. Oil of lavender is said to rejuvenate the skin of face and hands so that they look younger. At the least, it'll make you smell good!

LAVENDER COTTON

The feathery foliage of lavender cotton has a strong, musky scent that may help keep moths out of your woolens. The bright yellow button flowers may attract beneficial insects.

ALLIES: Lavender cotton, also known as santolina, is valued for its strongly scented foliage, which some companion gardeners believe repels insects.

COMPANIONS: Plant lavender cotton as a border to your vegetable garden or in masses in the ornamental garden. The tight growth of the plant makes it a good choice for herb garden hedges and knot gardens.

ENEMIES: None known.

GROWING GUIDELINES: Lavender cotton thrives in poor, light soil in full sun. Sow seed shallowly outdoors in late spring, or start with nursery-grown plants. Thin or space plants to stand 3 feet (90 cm) apart. Some companion gardeners feel that the yellow blooms detract from the form of the plant; snipping stems frequently will discourage flowering and promote dense, bushy growth.

COMMENTS: Lavender cotton is not related to lavender, but the gray-leaved plants share some resemblance. When they come into bloom, though, it's easy to see that these are two very different plants.

Lavender cotton is great as a backing for aromatic wreaths. Harvest when the flowers are in full bloom, snipping the leafy branches off about 6 inches (15 cm) from the ground; hang to dry. Green lavender cotton (*Santolina virens*) has bright green foliage and grows much like *S. chamaecyparissus;* the two complement each other nicely.

LEEK

Folklore recommends planting beets, broccoli, cabbage, cauliflower, summer savory, and tomatoes with leeks and its relatives (like onions and garlic).

ALLIES: Many companion gardeners are convinced that celery, onions, and carrots thrive when planted with leeks. Perhaps because of their oniony smell, leeks are also given the credit for repelling rust flies from carrots.

COMPANIONS: Compact, light-feeding leeks are easy to integrate anywhere in the garden.

ENEMIES: Companion gardeners believe that leeks inhibit the growth of peas and other legumes. Some believe sage and leeks do not thrive as neighbors.

GROWING GUIDELINES: Start seed in trays indoors 10–12 weeks before the average date of the last spring frost. Transplant seedlings into individual pots when they are large enough to handle. After frost has passed, when plants are about 8 inches (20 cm) tall, set them out into loose, fertile soil in full sun. Space them 6 inches (15 cm) apart, and plant them deeply so that only the top 2–3 inches (5–7.5 cm) of the leaves stick out. When the stems reach pencil size, mound the soil around the lower 2–3 inches (5–7.5 cm) to elongate the tender white stem base. Harvest after a light frost or two, or keep part of the crop for later digging.

COMMENTS: Leeks and other plants in the genus *Allium* (including onions) contain sulfur compounds that are believed to be fungicidal. Some companion gardeners mix up a home-brewed spray of puréed leeks and water for spritzing on diseased plants.

LEMON BALM

LETTUCE

The dainty white flowers of lemon balm attract so many honeybees that this plant is sometimes called the "bee herb." It is a good companion for all kinds of plants.

ALLIES: Perhaps because of its pleasing fragrance, lemon balm is said to benefit all vegetables. Planted with broccoli, cauliflower, or other members of the cabbage family, lemon balm may help to deter insects, perhaps by masking the cabbage smell.

COMPANIONS: Interplant with broccoli, cauliflower, and other cabbage-family crops. Grow lemon balm as a hedge around the orchard to attract bees for better pollination. Add to an ornamental border, or plant with roses.

ENEMIES: None known.

GROWING GUIDELINES: Sow seed, uncovered, in spring in average to lean, well-drained soil in full sun to light shade. Keep the seedbed moist until seeds germinate. Trim plants regularly to keep them bushy. Increase your supply with cuttings, layering, or division in spring or fall. Lemon balm also self-sows liberally.

COMMENTS: The aromatic leaves may have some effect as an insect repellent. Rub them on a picnic table to discourage flies, or brush yourself with a handful to keep away pesky mosquitoes.

Crisp, crunchy lettuce grows best in cool spring or fall weather. If you want to extend the season, combine lettuce with taller plants that can provide summer shade.

ALLIES: Many companion gardeners maintain that lettuce grows best when planted near or with strawberries, carrots, cucumbers, cabbage-family crops, and beets. Companion gardening tradition recommends planting lettuce with radishes for the mutual benefit of both crops. Scientific tests have shown that an intercrop of lettuce with cabbages reduces cabbage root flies; however, researchers have also tested both a companion crop of clover and an artificial green covering with the same results.

COMPANIONS: Plant lettuce below and around taller vegetables, such as cabbage, broccoli, and beans, or edge a bed with it. Interplant rows of leaf lettuce with rows of beans, peas, and tomatoes. Grow lettuce in containers or window boxes.

ENEMIES: None known.

GROWING GUIDELINES: Lettuce thrives in fertile, well-drained but moisture-retentive soil with plenty of organic matter. Sow seed in full sun as early as you can work the soil. Plant lettuce in rows, or broadcast the tiny seeds over a small patch. Sow as evenly as possible. Thin ruthlessly; you can always eat the thinnings. Allow 12–16 inches (30–40 cm) between plants for heading types; space plants 6–8 inches (15–20 cm) apart for leafy types. Water regularly to keep plants growing well, and side-dress with manure tea for rapid growth. Make a second and third planting 2 weeks apart to extend

LOVAGE

If you have the space, leave a row of lettuce to flower and set seed. Lettuce flowers attract a multitude of insects, including beneficials; birds relish the seeds.

Some companion gardeners claim that lovage improves the growth and flavor of pole and bush beans; it may also improve the flavor of other vegetable crops.

your lettuce harvest well into the summer. In areas with hot summers, look for heat-resistant cultivars such as 'Mantilia', 'Grand Rapids', and 'Summer Bibb'. Plant summer lettuce in the shade of bean trellises or other tall plants.

Harvest lettuce in the morning, when it is the most juicy and crispy. Pick leaf lettuce as needed. Press down on heading types to check for the springy firmness that indicates the head is ready to harvest. When plants start to elongate and send aloft a flowering stalk, the leaves become too bitter to enjoy. Keep the middle pinched out of your plants to discourage bolting and extend the harvest. Make a last sowing a month before the fall frost for a late crop.

COMMENTS: A salad of mixed greens is always more appealing than a bowl of plain 'Iceberg' lettuce. There are four basic lettuce types to choose from: leaf, butterhead, crisphead, and romaine. Leaf lettuce is easiest to grow; tender butterhead (also known as bibb or Boston lettuce) is a favorite of many salad-lovers.

ALLIES: Lovage is recommended as a trap crop to lure tomato hornworms away from tomatoes; handpick the pests or cut off and destroy infested foliage. The umbels of tiny greenish yellow flowers attract parasitic and predaceous insects to the garden, and the bushy plants provide shelter for predatory insects.

COMPANIONS: Lovage takes up quite a bit of room in the garden: A single plant may be all you need as a trap crop. Plant it at the back of the ornamental border for an eye-catching accent.

ENEMIES: None known.

GROWING GUIDELINES: This perennial herb can easily take the place of celery in recipes and is easier to grow. One plant is enough for most gardens. Sow seed shallowly in late summer or early fall, or purchase a young plant. Give lovage fertile, well-drained soil in full sun. Clip back young stems to encourage bushiness. Lovage dies back in winter; protect the roots with mulch. It is occasionally attacked by leafminers, so remove and destroy affected leaves.

COMMENTS: Leaves, stems, and seeds all have a savory celery-like flavor. Try the chopped leaves in potato salad and cream soups.

MARIGOLD

Marigolds have long been a tradition in the companion garden. Marigolds may repel some insects, but research has shown that they can also inhibit the growth of other plants.

A border of compact, colorful marigolds can give any garden a neat appearance. Pinch off spent flowers to promote bushier growth and the production of more flowers.

ALLIES: Marigolds have acquired a large body of companion gardening lore surrounding their reputed insect-repelling qualities. Companion gardeners suggest planting them with cabbage, potatoes, tomatoes, and roses, insisting that the pungently scented plants control aphids, cabbage loopers, imported cabbageworms, Mexican bean beetles, and nematodes. Only a few of the claims are backed up by scientific research, and sometimes the results are contradictory.

In addition, marigolds appear to have an allelopathic effect on some neighbors. In one study, French marigolds (*Tagetes patula*) repelled Mexican bean beetles, but the growth of the beans was stunted, apparently by the presence of the marigolds. One study on cabbageworm counts found that marigolds had no effect; in another, the number of worms was reduced but so was the size of the heads (apparently because of an allelopathic substance from the marigolds).

Nematode studies are more definitive, showing a decrease in population in at least five species of nematodes. Early studies focused on the resistance of marigolds to nematodes and found that the plants contain a potent nematocide that controlled meadow and root knot nematodes on infested land. Later studies showed that potato-root nematodes were unaffected or only slightly reduced by the toxin. Spectacular nematode control resulted when marigolds were interplanted with tomatoes, and similar results were shown with tobacco. Gardeners in India grow marigolds between beds of tomato-family vegetables such as potatoes, chili peppers, and eggplants, changing the layout year by year so that the whole garden area receives a dose of marigold nematocide.

COMPANIONS: Due to the possible allelopathic effects, it's probably best to plant marigolds and vegetables in separate beds. Grow the marigolds as a cover crop and turn them into the soil at the end of the season. The brightly colored flowers are always welcome in ornamental plantings.

ENEMIES: Marigolds appear to be allelopathic to beans and vegetables of the cabbage family.

GROWING GUIDELINES: Sow seed in lean to average soil with full sun after the last frost, or start with purchased plants. Space them 12–24 inches (30–60 cm) apart. At the end of the season, let a few seed heads mature and save the seed for next year.

COMMENTS: Mulches of marigold leaves have been effective in suppressing nematodes; root mulches are also repellent. These findings suggest that you might be better off tossing pulled-up marigolds on the garden rather than on the compost pile.

Origanum majorana   Labiatae

MARJORAM, SWEET

Sweet marjoram is a bushy, aromatic plant with a mild oregano taste. In summer, the plentiful clusters of tiny flowers attract many beneficial insects to the garden.

ALLIES: Companion gardeners recommend planting sweet marjoram to improve the growth and flavor of other nearby herbs.

COMPANIONS: Sweet marjoram can sprawl to cover a good-sized piece of ground; either prune it back or give it plenty of room. Plant with sage, chives, and other herbs, or add it to the flower garden. It also grows well in a container.

ENEMIES: None known.

GROWING GUIDELINES: The seeds are small and slow to germinate. If you want to try growing plants this way, sow seed shallowly indoors in spring. You can also buy plants at a garden center. Grow sweet marjoram in well-drained, average to lean soil in full sun. Cut back in late spring to keep the plant tidy and well branched; dry and store the clippings for seasoning. In summer, the bushy, branching plant is dotted with appealing clusters of tiny purple and pink flowers. After flowering, shear stems to 1 inch (2.5 cm) above the ground to produce vigorous new growth. Hang flower heads to dry for dried arrangements and wreaths. Sweet marjoram may self-sow in warm regions.

COMMENTS: This herb has a taste like mild oregano. Dried marjoram retains its flavor all winter. Sprinkle a handful of crushed leaves in scrambled eggs, potato soup, or eggplant dishes.

Cucumis spp. and other genera   Cucurbitaceae

MELONS

If you've got the space, there's nothing quite as rewarding as homegrown watermelons. Melons are heavy feeders, so work in plenty of compost or aged manure before planting.

ALLIES: Some companion gardeners recommend planting melons near corn and peas to improve melon growth and flavor. Peppery-leaved radishes and nasturtiums are sometimes recommended to deter cucumber beetles.

COMPANIONS: Interplant young melon seedlings with fast-growing radishes or beets to make good use of garden space early in the season. Sprawling melon vines also share ground successfully with sunflowers and corn.

ENEMIES: Folklore suggests that gourds and cucumbers make melons taste bitter. This is unlikely when the crops are grown together, although it can affect saved melon seeds; the melons might indeed have cross-pollinated with bitter-tasting gourds and cukes. Potatoes are said to stunt the growth of melons and reduce the yield.

GROWING GUIDELINES: Get a jump on the season by starting plants indoors. Sow seed ½ inch (12 mm) deep in individual peat pots 2–4 weeks before planting out. Wait to transplant seedlings to the garden until soil warms to at least 70°F (21°C); this is usually several weeks after the last frost. Plant pot and all to avoid disturbing roots (though you should remove the top rim of the peat pot or bury the rim entirely to keep it from drawing water away from the roots). Plant in hills of two or three plants in full sun, spacing hills as recommended

Mentha spp.   Labiatae

MINT

Follow or interplant fast-growing spring crops like radishes or lettuce with honeydew, crenshaw, and other long-season melons that need 3–4 warm months to mature.

on the seed packet. Apply fish emulsion when fruits set and repeat 2 weeks later.

Judging ripeness is a critical but tricky part of getting good melons. The stem of a ripe fruit usually will slip off easily, often as you pick up the melon. Lift the fruit to gauge ripeness of casabas, honeydews, and other melons; if the stem breaks cleanly with no pressure, the melon is ready. Thumping is a traditional but not always reliable test for watermelons; a dull, deadened sound means the melon is ripe or overripe. Check the bottom of a watermelon—if it has a definite yellow, gold, or orange hue, it's ready to pick; a pale yellow color usually means the melon is still unripe.

COMMENTS: Minimize problems by planting only disease-resistant cultivars. 'Ambrosia Hybrid' and 'Iroquois' muskmelons and 'Amber' honeydew are resistant to powdery mildew, a common problem in areas with high humidity. 'Delicious 51' and 'Honey-bush' muskmelons and 'Charleston Gray' and 'Jubilee' watermelons are resistant to Fusarium wilt, an all-too-common disease spread by the striped cucumber beetle.

Spearmint and peppermint, some say, will repel ants on plants or in the kitchen. Lay sprigs in drawers and on shelves. Mints may also protect woolens from moth damage.

ALLIES: These strong-smelling plants are favorites with companion gardeners who believe that the sharp fragrance repels insect pests. Some believe that mint also improves the vigor and flavor of cabbage and tomatoes. The flowers attract many beneficial insects.

COMPANIONS: Mint is notoriously invasive, so don't allow it free rein in your garden. If you want to grow mint around your crops, plant it in pots and set the pots near the plants you want to protect. Place a saucer beneath the pot to prevent the roots from creeping into the garden soil.

ENEMIES: None known.

GROWING GUIDELINES: Grow mint in average soil in full sun or partial shade. Extra moisture will encourage more vigorous growth. Buy plants or beg a cutting from a friend or neighbor to start your patch; mint cuttings are extremely easy to root. Lay the clipping horizontally on the surface of average to lean soil in full sun, and cover it in a few places with about $1/2$ inch (12 mm) of patted-down soil. Keep the soil moist until vigorous new growth appears, usually in just a few weeks. Seed-grown mint may or may not have a strong scent; rub a leaf and sniff before buying potted garden-center mints to make sure you are getting what you want.

COMMENTS: Mint oil may have fungicidal or pest-repellent uses; try a homemade spray (see "Herbal Sprays" on page 86 for directions).

| *Brassica* spp. | Cruciferae | *Tropaeolum majus* | Tropaeolaceae |

MUSTARD

NASTURTIUM

Science confirms much of traditional companion planting lore about mustard. Cultivated species can benefit many crops; wild mustard may be helpful or harmful.

Companion gardeners suggest nasturtiums as a trap crop for aphids; destroy infested plants. If you're growing nasturtiums as ornamentals, control pests with soap spray.

ALLIES: According to some studies, mustard deters flea beetles and aphids from collards and brussels sprouts. Brussels sprouts and collards intercropped with wild mustard had fewer cabbage aphids; collards had fewer flea beetles. Cultivated and weedy mustard species are reputed to improve the vigor of beans, grapevines, and fruit trees.

COMPANIONS: Grow mustard as a border or strip planting in gardens, orchards, or vineyards.

ENEMIES: Gardening lore recommends keeping mustard plants away from turnips. Wild mustard may bring more troubles to the garden than it prevents. It hosts insect pests, such as pea aphids, and may attract cutworms and other pests that will then move on to cabbage and other garden crops. Some studies indicate an allelopathic reaction from wild mustard that can stunt the growth of lettuce and other neighboring plants. It's probably best to confine your mustard plantings to cultivated types, and pull and destroy wild ones that crop up.

GROWING GUIDELINES: Mustard is easy to grow from seed in early spring or mid- to late-summer. Sow seed 1/2 inch (12 mm) deep, 3 inches (7.5 cm) apart, in average, well-drained soil in full sun. Thin to 6 inches (15 cm) apart; use the thinnings in soups and salads. Pull out flowering plants.

COMMENTS: Mustard's tang gets hotter as air temperatures rise. For mildest flavor, pick young leaves.

ALLIES: Nasturtiums are said to deter pests—including whiteflies—from beans, cabbage and its relatives, and cucumbers. Some companion gardeners plant nasturtiums where they will later plant their squash, hoping to keep squash bugs away. Scientific trials show conflicting evidence. In some tests, pests are reduced; in others, the nasturtiums had no effect, or worse, appeared to draw pests to the garden. It's worth conducting your own field trials.

COMPANIONS: Nasturtiums are available in compact or trailing forms. They flower well in poor soil and tend to produce more leaves than flowers if you plant them in the rich soil of the vegetable garden. Trailing types are pretty in a window box with marigolds and other annuals.

ENEMIES: None known.

GROWING GUIDELINES: Nasturtiums grow and flower best in average to poor soil. Plant seed 1/2 inch (12 mm) deep in full sun in well-drained soil after danger of frost has passed. Thin or space plants to stand 6–12 inches (15–30 cm) apart. Mulching and watering will encourage blooms during hot weather.

COMMENTS: The colorful, spurred flowers attract hummingbirds.

Hibiscus esculentus　　　　　　Malvaceae

OKRA

Besides producing edible pods, okra also makes an interesting ornamental. It thrives anywhere corn does, and its pods are attacked by corn earworms; handpick these pests.

ALLIES: If nematodes are a problem in your garden, plant the whole bed with marigolds the season before you plant okra. In an Indian study, the okra followed a planting of African marigolds (*Tagetes erecta*) and showed improved vigor and yields and less evidence of root-knot damage from nematodes.

COMPANIONS: This big plant takes up a lot of garden space, but lower-growing plants like eggplants and bell peppers can grow in its shade. Okra also makes an unusual ornamental, with showy flowers of white or creamy yellow. Try 'Burgundy', with red-tinged leaves and stems and pale yellow flowers.

ENEMIES: None known.

GROWING GUIDELINES: Wait until the soil is thoroughly warm before sowing seed; it will rot at cooler temperatures. Sow in full sun, spacing 3 inches (7.5 cm) apart and eventually thinning to 12–18 inches (30–45 cm) apart. Harvest 4–6 days after the flowers first bloom, when pods are 1–4 inches (2.5–10 cm) long. Wear gloves to protect your hands from the irritating spines on the pods, or plant a spineless cultivar such as 'Blondy'. Compact cultivars, such as 'Annie Oakley', are available.

COMMENTS: A leafhopper detrimental to cotton will also feed on okra; if you are raising a small cotton patch, try an okra border as a trap crop. Destroy infested plants.

Allium cepa　　　　　　Amaryllidaceae

ONION

Onions have a narrow, upright habit and shallow roots, so they're easy to squeeze in anywhere in the garden. Try planting onions around rose bushes to deter pests.

ALLIES: Onions interplanted with potatoes are believed to deter Colorado potato beetles. Some companion gardeners plant onions with carrots to fend off carrot rust flies that cause root maggots.

COMPANIONS: Interplant them with annual or perennial vegetables or use as borders to edge a bed.

ENEMIES: Peas, beans, and sage are the traditional bad neighbors for onions.

GROWING GUIDELINES: Use bulbs, or "sets," for interplanting—they are easy to pop into the ground, singly or in handfuls, wherever you want them. You can also grow onions from seed. Sow seed $1/2$ inch (12 mm) deep in loose, fertile soil in full sun; thin seedlings to stand about 1 inch (2.5 cm) apart. Thin again 4 weeks later so that plants stand 6 inches (15 cm) apart. Using your hand or working carefully with a hoe, scoop off a bit of soil, exposing the top of the bulb; this will encourage the bulb to fatten up.

If you start with a bundle or flat of seedlings, set them out 2 inches (5 cm) deep and 6 inches (15 cm) apart. Many companion gardeners plant sets one by one, pointed-side up, but if you are sowing a lot of onions for eating green and don't mind crooked stems, you can simply pour the sets from the bag into the row. Cover them with 1 inch (2.5 cm) of soil and firm the surface; the new shoots will right themselves.

OREGANO

Some gardeners believe that onions thrive with cabbage, beets, strawberries, and lettuce. Winter or summer savory planted nearby is said to improve the flavor of onions.

When onion tops yellow, knock them over. Dig the bulbs when the tops turn brown. Dry them in the sun in rows, laying the first row in all one direction and the next row in the opposite direction. Lay the tops of the second row over the bulbs of the first row to prevent sunscald. When skins are completely dry, wipe off the soil, remove the tops, and store the bulbs in a cool, airy spot. You can also keep the dried tops on and braid the onions for storage.

COMMENTS: Select a cultivar best suited to your gardening climate and season length; check seed catalogs for recommendations. 'Yellow Globe Danvers' is a good choice for all regions. 'White Sweet Spanish' is best in the North and West; 'Southport White Globe' is ideal for Southern gardens. If you garden in a short-season area, choose an early-maturing cultivar, such as 'Early Yellow Globe' or 'Crystal White Wax'.

A spray made from steeped onion skins may be effective against thrips (see "Herbal Sprays" on page 86 for directions). Sprays of onions and its relatives (including garlic) are also believed to have fungicidal properties.

Like other strongly aromatic herbs, oregano has gained a reputation with companion gardeners as a general pest repellent. Recommended companions include beans and peppers.

ALLIES: Oregano's plentiful clusters of dainty pink-purple flowers attract butterflies and beneficial insects. Mud dauber wasps, which carry caterpillars of all kinds to their paper nests as food for a growing brood of larvae, are frequent customers at oregano-flower feasts.

COMPANIONS: Interplant perennial oregano at permanent spots in the vegetable garden, or use it as a border. Oregano can also be attractive in flower beds.

ENEMIES: None known.

GROWING GUIDELINES: Buy plants to make sure you are planting the traditional, sharp-flavored oregano; some have very little flavor. Wild oregano (*O. vulgare*) is a sprawler and usually doesn't have much of that signature peppery flavor; it does produce bountiful flowers for wreaths and dried arrangements. Sow seed shallowly in a nursery bed in early summer. Pinch and sniff to find the most potent seedlings, and pull out and discard the rest. Transplant the saved seedlings to a permanent spot in average to lean soil in full sun. Space clumps 18–24 inches (45–60 cm) apart.

COMMENTS: For true oregano taste, look for plants of *O. vulgare* subsp. *hirtum,* also sold as *O. heracleoticum.* Often called Greek oregano, it is lower growing and less cold hardy, with a much sharper flavor.

Petroselinum crispum   Umbelliferae

PARSLEY

Asparagus, roses, and tomatoes are all said to benefit from nearby parsley plantings. Parsley's bright green leaves also make an attractive edging for any garden.

ALLIES: Many companion gardeners are convinced that parsley repels asparagus beetles. Others believe that parsley reduces carrot rust flies and beetles on roses. Interplanted parsley may also help invigorate tomatoes.

COMPANIONS: Rosettes of curly green parsley add a neat, old-fashioned touch to all kinds of garden beds. Plant parsley around the base of roses.

ENEMIES: None known.

GROWING GUIDELINES: Parsley is notoriously slow to germinate—according to an old homily, the seeds go to the devil and back seven times before breaking through the soil. Buy young plants, or sow seed shallowly in spring. Grow parsley in full sun or light shade in well-drained, average soil. After the new plant is established, harvest sprigs as needed. Parsley blooms in its second year and sometimes self-sows if you let a few seed heads stand.

COMMENTS: Dried parsley quickly loses flavor. Save a winter's worth of this versatile herb by chopping and freezing in zippered plastic bags. In order to attract beneficial insects to the garden, let a few plants flower and go to seed. Tiny parasitic wasps are especially fond of the very small flowers, which are clustered together in umbels.

Pastinaca sativa   Umbelliferae

PARSNIP

Long grown for their sweet roots, parsnips have escaped the confines of the garden and are found across America as a roadside weed. They will flower their second year from seed.

ALLIES: Some people believe that parsnips grow better if you plant them near peas.

COMPANIONS: The deep roots grow long and straight in lean soil. Plant them with other annual crops, such as peas and other legumes, that prefer a soil that's not too rich.

ENEMIES: None known.

GROWING GUIDELINES: Plant parsnips in full sun in loose, average, well-drained soil. Prepare the bed as you would for carrots, taking care to remove rocks, stones, and other obstacles to root growth. Pulverize hard lumps of soil, and loosen the soil by digging in compost.

Sow seed $1/2$–1 inch (1–2 cm) deep as early as the ground can be worked. Soak seed to hasten germination. Parsnip seed is temperamental; many seeds will not sprout. Sow thickly, and thin as necessary to 8 inches (20 cm) apart. A few frosts will improve the flavor of the roots. You can dig them as long as the soil remains unfrozen. Store like carrots—in a box of damp, loose sand.

COMMENTS: The long, large roots of parsnip have a sweetly nutty flavor that lends itself well to savory winter soups and stews. Some companion gardeners use a spray made from parsnip foliage or roots as a mild insecticide (see "Herbal Sprays" on page 86 for directions).

| *Pisum sativum* | Leguminosae | *Prunus persica* | Rosaceae |

PEA

PEACH

A weedy garden may benefit your pea crop. Researchers found that white mustard shelters a pea aphid parasite; weeds also offer egg-laying sites for helpful hover flies.

Some companion gardeners believe that a planting of garlic close to peach tree trunks repels borers. Strawberries have proven to be another good companion for peaches.

ALLIES: Companion gardeners believe this nitrogen-fixing legume stimulates the growth of corn, beans, potatoes, tomatoes, radishes, carrots, turnips, and cucumbers. Scientific research indicates that exudates from the roots of cabbage-family crops may help prevent pea root rot.

COMPANIONS: Grow tomatoes, eggplants, lettuce, or spinach in the shade of trellised pea plants. The pea vines also protect these tender crops from wind damage. Alternate rows of peas with shade-tolerant Chinese cabbage.

ENEMIES: Onions and garlic are reputed to have a negative effect on the growth of peas.

GROWING GUIDELINES: Peas thrive in average, well-drained soil in full sun. Sow seed 1 inch (2.5 cm) deep in early spring, up to 2 months before the last expected frost. Some gardeners start peas indoors in individual peat pots. Thin or space plants to stand 3 inches (7.5 cm) apart. Mulch to control weeds and keep the soil evenly moist. Give plants a trellis to climb, or let short-vining cultivars trail on the ground. After you harvest an early crop of peas, remove the vines and plant squash, beans, or other crops to utilize the space.

COMMENTS: Pea greens are an oriental delicacy. Plant an extra row of peas and leave them unthinned to supply your kitchen with these tasty, delicate greens.

ALLIES: Strawberries are alternate hosts of a parasite that attacks oriental fruit moths, a common peach pest; researchers noted reduced populations of these destructive moths when strawberries were growing nearby. Weeds and grass harbor parasitic and predacious insects that attack red spider mites, another pest of peach trees; unfortunately, they may also increase borer populations.

COMPANIONS: Plant annual vegetables or herbs around and between the trees while they are young. Use strawberries as a cover crop, border, or strip planting near peaches.

ENEMIES: Peaches are susceptible to Verticillium wilt; don't plant them where potatoes, raspberries, tomatoes, or other wilt carriers once grew. As with other members of the rose family, peaches fail to thrive if planted in the "grave" of an old tree. Plant a new tree elsewhere to avoid pathogens that may be in the soil.

GROWING GUIDELINES: Plant young, dormant trees in spring in well-drained soil with a pH of 6.0–6.5. Most cultivars are self-pollinating. To avoid frost damage, plant near the top of a slope. Mulch with compost to keep the soil evenly moist.

COMMENTS: Peach trees are seldom long-lived; plan on a 12-year life span, and start replacements ahead of time. Select a disease-resistant cultivar, and buy only certified disease-free stock.

Arachis hypogaea   Leguminosae   *Capsicum frutescens,* Grossum group   Solanaceae

PEANUT   # PEPPER

Peanuts need a warm growing season of at least 4 months. Northern gardeners should start the seed indoors; Southern gardeners can direct-sow around the last frost.

ALLIES: Research on field crops indicates that peanuts may increase the yield of other crops. Their presence has been shown in another study to increase the population of predatory spiders.

COMPANIONS: Interplant bushy peanuts with larger garden vegetables like corn and squash.

ENEMIES: None known.

GROWING GUIDELINES: Plant seed 4 weeks before the last spring frost, in a 3-inch (7.5 cm) round peat pot. Transplant the seedlings to the garden, in loose, fertile, well-drained soil in full sun, when the soil is well warmed. Space plants 10 inches (25 cm) apart. Some researchers report high yields without thinning, but most gardeners thin direct-sown seedlings to stand 10–12 inches (25–30 cm) apart. As the peanut plant matures, flowering stalks called peduncles bend downward, growing into the soil, in a process known as "pegging." Peanuts form on the underground pegs. When the leaves turn yellow, pull up plants, shake off soil, and dry until leaves crumble. Remove the pods and boil, blanch, or roast the seeds.

COMMENTS: Peanuts, like other legumes, enrich the soil for future crops of other plants. Their roots form an association with certain bacteria in the soil; these bacteria work with the plant to capture nitrogen gas from the air and convert it into nitrogen compounds that plants can use.

Companion gardeners recommend planting peppers with carrots and onions for vigorous growth and good flavor. Basil, lovage, marjoram, and oregano may also stimulate growth.

ALLIES: Gardeners in India use marigolds to protect peppers and other crops from nematodes. Scientific studies indicate that marigolds are effective in reducing aphids on peppers; other strong-smelling plants, such as coriander, catnip, onions, nasturtiums, and tansy, may have the same effect.

COMPANIONS: Plant peppers with okra or other tall plants for protection from sun and wind damage.

ENEMIES: Some companion gardeners keep kohlrabi and fennel away from pepper plants. It's best to keep peppers away from beans; both are susceptible to anthracnose, a disease that causes dark, soft spots on fruits. Weed regularly; related weeds such as deadly nightshade and groundcherries may be carriers of mosaic virus.

GROWING GUIDELINES: Buy nursery-grown seedlings, or start seed indoors in peat pots 8 weeks before the last spring frost. Give seedlings bottom heat, so that the soil temperature is about 75°F (24°C). Use a heating cable, which is sold at garden centers or in catalogs, for this purpose; you may also have success by placing the tray of pots on top of your refrigerator. Seeds are slow to germinate, often waiting 3–4 weeks to make an appearance. Thin to one plant per pot when they reach 3 inches (7.5 cm) high, snipping off the extras with a pair of small scissors. Transplant to fertile, well-drained soil in full sun, 2–3 weeks after the last spring frost.

PETUNIA

Peppers often drop their blossoms in temperatures over 80°F (30°C); keep them cool by growing with taller plants that will provide some shade in the hottest part of the day.

Plant petunias as a vegetable garden border, or grow some near your favorite summer sitting spot and watch for hummingbird-like sphinx moths visiting the blossoms at dusk.

Space plants 1¹/₂–2 feet (45–60 cm) apart; hot peppers tolerate closer spacing than sweet peppers. Mulch to maintain even moisture, and water during dry spells to prevent bitterness. A dose of fish emulsion when plants are in flower can help increase yields. Sweet peppers turn from green to red, yellow, or purple as they mature, getting sweeter with the color change; pick at any stage. Hot peppers also change color when it's time to pick. Dry peppers whole, or chop and freeze them in zippered plastic bags. No blanching is necessary. Wear rubber gloves when handling hot peppers, and do not touch your fingers to your eyes or mouth—the juice can cause a burning sensation.

COMMENTS: Hot pepper spray is a traditional gardening insect repellent, and anecdotal evidence suggests it is effective against a number of pests. Peppers themselves may be prone to aphids; a spray of aromatic herbs or garlic may deter these pests. See "Herbal Sprays" on page 86 for information on preparing these sprays.

ALLIES: Some companion gardeners intercrop petunias with beans, squash, and potatoes in the belief that the petunias will control squash bugs, Mexican bean beetles, and potato bugs. Scientific trials with beans failed to confirm this, but another study indicated that petunias may help control tobacco hornworms.

COMPANIONS: Use petunias as a border around vegetable beds, especially raised beds, where the flowering stems can trail over the sides.

ENEMIES: None known.

GROWING GUIDELINES: Petunias are slow to grow to blooming size from seed; sow indoors in late winter. If you don't want to bother with the tiny seeds, choose from the many flower types and colors that are available at garden centers. Plant in average, well-drained soil in full sun. Rejuvenate lanky plants by nipping the trailing stems in half to encourage new lateral growth. Petunias often put on a new show of flowers when days shorten near fall.

COMMENTS: Let hybrid petunias self-sow for a pleasant surprise: What comes up next spring will bear only the slightest resemblance to the parents. Big-blossomed hybrids revert to old-fashioned smaller, single flowers in quiet pinks, lavenders, and whites. Best of all, self-sown petunias often have outstanding fragrance. They'll resow year after year.

POTATO

To improve the growth and flavor of your next potato crop, many companion gardeners recommend interplanting with beans, cabbage, corn, or horseradish.

For easy-to-harvest potatoes, cover planted pieces with layers of loose compost, leaves, or straw; at harvest time, simply pull the tubers out of the mulch.

ALLIES: Companion gardeners often recommend marigolds to ward off pests and sometimes plant eggplants as a trap crop for Colorado potato beetles. Tests at the Rodale Research Center in Pennsylvania with plantings of catnip, coriander, nasturtium, and tansy resulted in a slightly reduced infestation of beetle larvae. According to one study, tomato-family weeds such as jimson weed and deadly nightshade attract female Colorado potato beetles away from the crop to lay their eggs on the weeds, especially when the weeds are growing upwind.

COMPANIONS: Plant lettuce, radishes, and green onions with potatoes; they mature long before the tuber crop is ready to dig.

ENEMIES: Companion gardeners say potatoes may be more susceptible to blight if grown near raspberries, pumpkins, tomatoes, squash, cucumbers, and sunflowers.

GROWING GUIDELINES: Potatoes thrive in loose, fertile, well-drained soil in full sun. Cut whole potatoes into pieces, each with two or three "eyes" (growing points), and let them dry for a day before planting. Plant the pieces as soon as you can work the soil, spacing them 6–12 inches (15–30 cm) apart and 4 inches (10 cm) deep. As the vines grow, pull soil over the developing tubers to prevent them from turning green, or cover them with compost, leaves, or straw. Some companion gardeners grow potatoes in cages; fill the cage with straw as the plants grow, leaving only 3–4 inches (7.5–10 cm) of leaves exposed.

Blossoms are a sign that new potatoes are ready to harvest. Uncover a layer and pluck off tubers that are big enough to eat; cover the rest. When the tops of the plants begin to die back, it's harvest time. Potatoes will keep in the ground for several weeks. If you've planted in straw or loose compost, grab the plant and pull up—roots, tubers, and all. Plants in garden soil may require some digging to collect the crop. Set aside nicked or damaged tubers, and eat those first.

COMMENTS: Garden catalogs are full of out-of-the-ordinary cultivars. Try buttery-tasting, yellow-fleshed 'Yellow Finn' or an old reliable like 'Kennebec'. "Mini" tubers of some cultivars are also available for starting a crop. Instead of cut pieces, these starters are whole, small tubers, $1/2$–$1^1/2$ inches (12–37 mm) in diameter, and certified disease-free. Each tuber produces at least 3 pounds (1.5 kg) of full-sized potatoes. Seed for potatoes has also appeared on the market; it produces 4-inch (10 cm) tubers in just 90 days. Even that sprouted bag of potatoes in the kitchen cabinet can yield a decent crop. Dump them into a soft bed of soil and separate them with a hoe; cover them with soil or straw.

| *Cucurbita pepo* | Cucurbitaceae | *Raphanus sativus* | Cruciferae |

PUMPKIN

RADISH

If you want to win the big-pumpkin contest, plant flowers like borage and lemon balm near the patch; research shows that pumpkins pollinated by numerous bees form bigger fruits.

Radish seeds are so quick to sprout that you can sow them with slower-germinating crops (like carrots) to mark the rows. Radishes are ready to pick in as little as 3 weeks.

ALLIES: None known.

COMPANIONS: American Indians have been planting pumpkins with corn, beans, and sunflowers for thousands of years. Tall corn and sunflowers provide shade from the hot summer sun for the growing arms of the pumpkin vine. A crop of beans, peas, or clover will enrich the soil for next year's crop.

ENEMIES: Pumpkins may be more susceptible to blight if grown near raspberries. Potatoes are said to inhibit the growth of the vines and fruit; pumpkins may have a similar effect on potatoes.

GROWING GUIDELINES: Pumpkins thrive in deep, rich soil in full sun. After the last expected frost, sow seed ¹/₂ inch (12 mm) deep, two or three seeds per hill, in hills 4–5 feet (1.2–1.5 m) apart. Mulch with compost; water with fish emulsion every 3–4 weeks. If vines stray out of their allotted space, nudge them gently and gradually where you want them to go. Harvest pumpkins after the vines have died. Light frosts won't hurt them, but bring in the crop if heavy frost is predicted. Cure them in the sun for 2 weeks.

COMMENTS: Children enjoy making a personalized pumpkin. Lightly carve initials or a name into the outer skin. As the pumpkin grows, it will heal the marks, leaving a raised scar in the shape of the name. If your garden space is limited, try space-saving bush types with extra-small pumpkins.

ALLIES: Some companion gardeners are convinced that radishes grown with peas and lettuce are more tender. Radishes are also said to thrive with beans, carrots, kohlrabi, parsnips, and onions. Nasturtiums and mustard are supposed to protect radishes from flea beetles. Radishes are reputed to repel striped cucumber beetles from cucumbers and prevent borers in squash and melons.

COMPANIONS: Intercrop radishes with other vegetables wherever there is open space for a few weeks.

ENEMIES: Some gardeners believe that radishes are harmful to grapevines. Hyssop is said to have a negative effect on radishes.

GROWING GUIDELINES: Sow radish seed ¹/₂ inch (12 mm) deep in average, well-drained garden soil, in full sun. In spring, start sowing as soon as you can work the soil (3–5 weeks before the last expected frost). Sow successive crops every 2 weeks until a month after the last frost. Thin to allow 2–4 inches (5–10 cm) between plants. Water frequently to keep the flavor from getting too hot. Summer heat will soon turn them woody and bitter; plant another crop in shade or wait for cooler fall weather. Sow fall crops starting 8 weeks before the first expected fall frost and continuing until frost.

COMMENTS: Radish is a member of the cabbage family; avoid planting cabbage, broccoli, and related crops where radishes last grew.

Rheum rhabarbatum   Polygonaceae

RHUBARB

Rosa spp.   Rosaceae

ROSE

Rhubarb leaves contain oxalic acid in amounts toxic to humans, but the plant makes a good neighbor to most other crops as long as you allow it plenty of space.

ALLIES: None known.

COMPANIONS: Although rhubarb is very big, it is not invasive and will stay where you put it. Give it a permanent planting site, keeping in mind that the large leaves may cast shade on nearby crops. Some gardeners are tempted to use rhubarb in ornamental plantings for foliage effect, but the leaves often have a tattered look by the end of the season.

ENEMIES: None known.

GROWING GUIDELINES: This dramatic plant grows best where the mean summer temperature is about 75°F (24°C) and the mean winter temperature is below 40°F (4.5°C). Buy dormant roots or potted plants in early spring to establish a new rhubarb bed. Plant in well-drained, fertile soil in full sun, setting roots so that the crown of the plant is just below the surface. Space clumps 4 feet (1.2 m) apart. Water well. Mulch deeply after the leaves appear. Wait until the second year after planting before harvesting the stalks. Cut out flower stalks as they appear to avoid slowing down leaf production.

COMMENTS: Thin leaf stalks are a sign that the plant needs to be divided. Wait until the following spring, then dig up the plant before leaves unfurl. Separate the crown into pieces, each with two or three buds; replant.

There are many natural controls that you can use against rose pests. Garlic oil is effective against Japanese beetles, aphids, and spider mites; it may also control diseases.

ALLIES: Alliums—including garlic, onions, leeks, and chives—are reputed to protect roses against black spot, mildew, and aphids. Parsley is said to repel rose beetles. Some companion gardeners suggest that strongly aromatic herbs may also repel aphids.

COMPANIONS: Low-growing plants, such as creeping thyme or sweet alyssum, make attractive groundcovers beneath rose bushes; these small-flowered plants may also attract beneficials to protect roses.

ENEMIES: As with all members of the rose family, never plant a new rose in an old rose's "grave": Disease pathogens or allelopathic substances that hinder the growth of a new plant of the same genus may be lurking in the soil.

GROWING GUIDELINES: Roses need at least 6 hours of sun each day, and they must have excellent drainage. They do best in fertile soil enriched with humus or other organic material. Dig the hole deep enough so the graft union—the scar on the stem that indicates where the rose has been budded onto its rootstock—is at or just below the soil surface. Trim canes back to 8 inches (20 cm), and mulch plants with compost. Prune off and destroy any diseased leaves or branches.

COMMENTS: Some gardeners use a spray made from solanine-containing tomato leaves, which they believe is an effective insecticide for rose pests (see "Herbal Sprays" on page 86 for directions).

Rosmarinus officinalis   Labiatae   *Ruta graveolens*   Rutaceae

ROSEMARY

RUE

Rosemary is a popular companion for cabbage, broccoli, and related crops, as well as carrots and onions. The small flowers will attract large numbers of bees.

Some gardeners suggest planting rue with figs or roses, though no scientific evidence supports the value of this. In fact, many plants seem to dislike rue as a companion.

ALLIES: The fragrance of rosemary is said to repel insects; companion gardeners use it for cabbage flies, root maggot flies, and other flying pests.

COMPANIONS: Gardeners in warm climates—especially the Pacific Southwest, where rosemary reaches shrub proportions—can enjoy this attractive, aromatic plant as a hedge or border. Prostrate types make beautiful groundcovers for stony banks or streetside rock gardens. Rosemary is a natural addition to herb gardens.

ENEMIES: None known.

GROWING GUIDELINES: Grow from cuttings or buy a started plant. This tender perennial often won't survive the winter in areas colder than Zone 7. Use as a pot plant in Northern gardens, or plant it out during summer and pot up cuttings for overwintering. In containers or in the garden, rosemary thrives on heat. Plant in full sun in average, well-drained soil. Never allow container plantings to dry out; rosemary does not recover from severe wilting.

COMMENTS: Rosemary has also won favor as a defense against clothes moths. Banckes wrote in his *Herbal:* "Take the flowers and put them in thy chest among thy clothes or among thy Bookes and Mothes shall not destroy them."

ALLIES: Rose growers sometimes recommend strong-smelling rue as a companion planting to repel insect pests.

COMPANIONS: The striking blue-green foliage of this perennial herb has an unusual and distinctive fragrance. Rue is a beautiful, eye-catching plant for the herb garden. It is also good in pots, especially terra cotta, which sets off the lacy gray-green foliage.

ENEMIES: Rue has a longer list of enemies than it does of partners, beginning with the gardener. Merely brushing against the plant can cause an unpleasant and painful contact dermatitis in susceptible individuals. Unfortunately, you won't know if you're susceptible until you experience the blistering rash. Some companion gardeners urge that you keep rue away from cabbage, broccoli, or other plants of the cabbage family. It is also said to inhibit the growth of culinary sage and basil.

GROWING GUIDELINES: Rue thrives in poor, well-drained soil in full sun. Buy nursery plants, or sow seed shallowly indoors in late winter. Transplant in late spring to stand 18–24 inches (45–60 cm) apart. Mulch with compost. Prune off dead stems in spring.

COMMENTS: Use the dried seedpods and leaves in flower arrangements. Folklore suggests using the herb to ward off the spells of witches.

Brassica napus, Napobrassica group   Cruciferae

RUTABAGA

For a good rutabaga crop, companion gardening lore suggests the same companions as for other members of the cabbage family: celery, onions, and potatoes.

ALLIES: Aromatic plants, including marigolds, nasturtiums, pennyroyal, peppermint, sage, and thyme, are reputed to repel pests around cabbage-family crops; in one scientific study, however, nasturtiums actually attracted cabbage flea beetles. Studies have shown that marigolds do reduce pest infestations, but they also have caused allelopathic reactions with cabbage and may have the same effect on rutabagas and other related crops.

COMPANIONS: Alternating rows of rutabagas with tomatoes may give some protection from whiteflies and flea beetles. In fertile soil, interplant rutabagas with other heavy-feeding cabbage-family crops.

ENEMIES: Gardening tradition recommends keeping all plants of the cabbage family away from grapevines.

GROWING GUIDELINES: Rutabagas grow best in loose, fertile soil in full sun. Sow seed ¹/₂ inch (12 mm) deep about 14 weeks before the first fall frost date. Thin new seedlings to 1 inch (2.5 cm) apart; thin again 2 weeks later to 8 inches (20 cm). Apply a heavy mulch to keep roots cool. Rutabagas need cool nights to develop flavor. Harvest when they are at least 3 inches (7.5 cm) across.

COMMENTS: Long-keeping rutabagas are a great crop for winter storage. Try them mashed and buttered or simmered in soups and stews. Munch on thin slices for a low-calorie snack.

Secale cereale   Gramineae

RYE

*Grown as a cover crop and turned into the soil, winter rye can help suppress the growth of quack grass (*Agropyron repens*), a pesky, spreading perennial weed.*

ALLIES: A sprinkling of cornflowers (*Centaurea cyanus*) in a rye field is said to improve its growth.

COMPANIONS: Rye is usually grown by itself. It is a common cover crop in many garden beds; the thick, fast growth crowds out weeds.

ENEMIES: Research indicates that decomposing rye plants release a toxin that inhibits the growth of some plants. Researchers tested the effect on weeds, tobacco, and lettuce; the toxins stunted growth and in some cases caused discolored lesions. It is still unknown what effect decomposing residues of a green manure or cover crop of rye may have on other garden vegetables.

GROWING GUIDELINES: Sow annual winter rye in late summer or fall for a winter cover crop. Mix with clover for a nitrogen-rich planting. In early summer of the following year, turn under the rye as a green manure. For a grain crop, sow in late summer to late fall, broadcasting at about 4 pounds per 1,000 square feet (2 kg per 93 sq m). Spread a loose straw mulch after seeding. Harvest when you can dent but not squash kernels with a fingernail.

COMMENTS: Hull rye kernels with a two-step process: Spread them on a cookie sheet and heat in the oven at 180°F (80°C) for 1 hour. Then process the toasted kernels, ¹/₄ cup at a time, in a blender, using short pulses. Pour into a shallow bowl and pick out the hulls by hand.

SAGE

SAVORY, SUMMER

Many companion gardeners believe that sage improves the growth and flavor of cabbage, carrots, strawberries, and tomatoes; it is also thought to grow well with marjoram.

ALLIES: Some companion gardeners believe that sage deters cabbage-family pests such as imported cabbageworms and root maggot flies. In one study, cabbageworms were not reduced by companion plantings with sage; another study of sage spray revealed some effectiveness in controlling the pest.

COMPANIONS: The plentiful, usually blue, flowers of this perennial herb are attractive to bees and other insects, including beneficials. Use sage as a border planting, or dot the plants among annual or perennial vegetables; they grow to an appreciable size in just one season.

ENEMIES: Sage is thought to stunt the growth of cucumbers. Many companion gardeners believe that sage and rue make poor neighbors. Long ago, people believed that sage and onions had a negative effect on each other in the garden.

GROWING GUIDELINES: Sage needs full sun and average, well-drained soil. Sow seed shallowly indoors in late winter or outdoors in late spring. Space plants about 24 inches (60 cm) apart. Trim back drastically in early spring to encourage vigorous, bushy new growth. Plants may decline after several years; take cuttings or divide in spring or fall to have a steady supply.

COMMENTS: A branch of strongly aromatic sage is a fragrant addition to a sweater drawer or blanket chest, and it may help keep clothes moths away.

Summery savory is a popular choice for companion planting with beans. Some gardeners claim that this herb improves the flavor of beans; it may also deter bean beetles.

ALLIES: Many companion gardeners recommend companion plantings of savory, both summer and winter, for giving onions a mild sweetness.

COMPANIONS: This bushy annual reaches about 1 foot (30 cm) high. Use it as a border or interplant with annual vegetables. Savory bears many small flowers much appreciated by bees; Virgil recommended a planting near beehives to flavor the honey.

ENEMIES: None known.

GROWING GUIDELINES: Summer savory sprouts fast from fresh seed. Sow shallowly in pots in spring. When these seedlings reach a manageable size, transplant them to average, well-drained soil in full sun, spacing about 10 inches (25 cm) apart. Snip off the tips of branches to use fresh in cooking. When the plant flowers, clip off the stems just above the ground and lay them on a screen tray to dry. Crumble leaves and store in tightly closed jars for winter use. Let a plant stand to self-sow for next year.

COMMENTS: Summer savory has a taste similar to thyme, with a bit of pepper bite. Known to many people as "the bean herb," summer savory improves the flavor of all bean dishes and has some reputation as an antiflatulent. Try dried savory in winter bean soups, or use fresh, finely chopped leaves with fish or in gazpacho. Mash a few leaves into butter for an interesting taste on hearty breads.

Satureja montana Labiatae

SAVORY, WINTER

Winter savory is more strongly aromatic than summer savory, and that quality has given it a reputation as an insect repellent in both the garden and the home.

ALLIES: Some companion gardeners plant the herb with beans and cabbage in the hope of deterring pests. Research so far has shown no effect on cabbage pests or whiteflies. Winter savory is also said to improve the flavor and growth of onions.

COMPANIONS: Winter savory, a perennial, is lower growing than its summer cousin. Its thin leaves are a glossy dark green, adding some contrast to herb garden plantings. Plant it near the kitchen door, so it's in easy reach for cooking. The leaves hold well into winter, so you can snip them as needed, sometimes even at Christmastime.

ENEMIES: None known.

GROWING GUIDELINES: Winter savory seed can be slow to sprout. Sow seed shallowly in pots in spring or buy a young plant. Give winter savory well-drained soil in full sun; it may rot over winter in heavy clay. Space plants 12 inches (30 cm) apart. Take cuttings or divide clumps in spring or fall.

COMMENTS: Winter savory has a strong, almost pine-like fragrance. Use it with strong-tasting meats or fish. Old-time herbals recommended adding dried, crushed winter savory to breadings for "meate." Savory is sometimes used to repel moths from the clothes closet.

Artemisia abrotanum Compositae

SOUTHERNWOOD

Grow southernwood as a pest-repelling border, or interplant it in permanent spots throughout the vegetable garden and orchard. This perennial also makes a nice hedge.

ALLIES: Many companion gardeners recommend interplanting southernwood as a kind of living insect repellent. Planted among beans, it is said to deter black aphids; near broccoli, cabbage, and related crops it is reputed to repel cabbage moths and other pests. The herb is also said to deter codling moths from orchard fruit.

COMPANIONS: Use this perennial herb throughout the garden. Keep a healthy specimen in a container as a portable insect repellent; the sharp, lemony scent is pleasant on a deck or patio. Bruise the leaves to release the essential oils.

ENEMIES: Unlike wormwood, its more unpleasantly scented relative, southernwood is not generally believed to harm the growth of any plant.

GROWING GUIDELINES: Southernwood is very difficult to grow from seed, but cuttings root easily. Snip a few from a friend's plant or buy a young potted plant. Grow in average, well-drained soil in full sun. Do not fertilize; southernwood prefers a lean diet. Prune back hard in spring.

COMMENTS: Harvest and dry the branches for use in wreaths and arrangements. The dried foliage may also be useful for repelling moths from stored clothing. Southernwood was once used as an aphrodisiac and was known as both "lad's love" and "maid's ruin."

Glycine max   Leguminosae

SOYBEAN

Soybeans are easy to grow from seed and are mostly untroubled by pests. Look for cultivars developed especially for home use, such as 'Prize' and 'Okuhara'.

ALLIES: According to both companion gardeners and scientists, plantings of soybeans and corn benefit each other. Studies show that the nitrogen-fixing root nodules of the beans grow larger when interplanted with corn. Volatile compounds from soybean plants were shown to stimulate the uptake of phosphorus by corn plants. Soybeans are also a valuable intercrop with wheat, say researchers.

COMPANIONS: Alternate double rows of corn with double rows of soybeans. Plant a heavy-feeding crop like cabbage the year after a soybean planting to take advantage of the increased nitrogen.

ENEMIES: None known.

GROWING GUIDELINES: Sow in spring after the soil has warmed or in early summer. Plant seed 1 inch (2.5 cm) deep and 2 inches (5 cm) apart in average, well-drained soil in full sun. Thin to 6 inches (15 cm). Soybean plants are bushy and sprawling, with small purple flowers. When pods fill out, harvest the green beans to eat fresh. For dried beans to use in winter soups and stews, let the pods dry on the vine until the beans rattle.

COMMENTS: Steam plump green soybeans, pods and all; drizzle with lemon, then squeeze the pods to pop the nutritious, nutty-flavored beans into your mouth. The ripened stems of golden pods are a nice addition to dried arrangements.

Spinacia oleracea   Cruciferae

SPINACH

Spinach prefers the cool weather of spring or fall, though it will grow into the summer if you shade it with taller plants, like a row of trellised peas.

ALLIES: Spinach is often recommended as a companion crop to celery, eggplants, cabbage, peas, and onions, probably more because of its growth habit than because of any "beneficial" qualities.

COMPANIONS: Underplant taller vegetable crops and fill empty spaces in the beds with fast-growing, fast-sprouting spinach. Sow a few spinach seeds around or beneath each plant of brussels sprouts, cabbage, eggplant, peppers, and celery.

ENEMIES: None known.

GROWING GUIDELINES: Spinach thrives in sun or light shade in deep, loose, fertile soil that is well drained but moisture-retentive. Sow seed ¹/₂ inch (12 mm) deep in early spring as soon as you can work the soil (usually 3–5 weeks before the last expected frost). Make successive plantings every few weeks until early summer for a continuous harvest. Spinach quickly goes to flower in hot weather; sow the last spring planting in shade, or wait until mid- to late-summer to sow a fall crop. Thin plants to 6 inches (15 cm) apart when young. Mulch with compost. Remove and destroy any leaves disfigured by leafminers, or protect plants with floating row covers.

COMMENTS: You can enjoy a spinach salad long into fall and sometimes winter if you blanket the row with a thick layer of loosely piled leaves.

SQUASH

Squash, one of the American Indians' "three sisters," is traditionally grown with corn and beans. Tall sunflowers are another useful companion crop for squash.

Summer squashes grow fast, so pick the fruit every few days, while it is still young and tender. Harvest winter squash when the shell is too hard to dent with a fingernail.

ALLIES: Some companion gardeners recommend a nearby planting of radishes, nasturtiums, or mint and other aromatic herbs to repel insect pests such as squash bugs. Studies at the Rodale test gardens have shown a possible reduction of squash bugs on zucchini paired with catnip or tansy.

COMPANIONS: Summer squash, such as crookneck and zucchini, grow on bushy, nonvining plants. Winter squash, such as acorn, butternut, and Hubbard, produce very long vines. Plant both kinds with corn or sunflowers.

ENEMIES: Gardening lore suggests that squash plants may inhibit the growth of potatoes.

GROWING GUIDELINES: Squash thrives in fertile, well-drained soil in full sun. After the last frost, plant seed 1 inch (2.5 cm) deep when the soil has warmed. Space summer squash 1–2 feet (30–60 cm) apart; winter, 2–4 feet (60–120 cm) apart. You can also grow winter squash up sturdy trellises to save space; suspend ripening fruits in a panty-hose sling. Water with fish emulsion every 3–4 weeks. Mulch with straw to keep the soil moist. Gently guide straying vines back where they belong.

COMMENTS: Squash are susceptible to various pests and ailments that can cause serious damage. Watch for signs of trouble, like wilting vines, which can indicate squash borers or bacterial wilt; destroy infected plants. Insects spread disease by carrying spores from leaf to leaf. 'Sweet Mama', a buttercup-type winter squash, is resistant to Fusarium wilt and vine borers.

Before breeders began tinkering with them, many plants of the cucurbit family contained bitter, toxic substances called cucurbitacins. The plants developed these compounds to ward off predation, but specialized insects consider those very substances an open invitation. Cucurbitacins are very attractive to striped cucumber beetles (which feed on squash just as voraciously as they do on cucumbers). Fourteen cucurbitacins are known, and all but one have been shown in scientific trials to stimulate striped cucumber beetles into voracious eating.

Hybridizers, perhaps by breeding for better taste, have managed to eliminate most of the cucurbitacins from some cultivars of squash, melons, and cucumbers. Curiously, while cucumber beetles are less attracted to cucurbitacin-free cultivars, spider mites may be more apt to attack those plants.

Fragaria spp.   Rosaceae

STRAWBERRY

Gardening tradition suggests that your strawberry bed will thrive when planted near or interplanted with crops like beans, borage, lettuce, and spinach.

ALLIES: Many companion gardeners insist that the herb borage improves the flavor and the yield of a strawberry crop. "Among strawberries here and there sow some Borage seed and you shall find the strawberries fare much larger than their fellows," wrote William Coles some 350 years ago.

COMPANIONS: Use strawberries around peach trees; the plants are an alternate host for a parasitic insect that preys on oriental fruit moths, a pest of peach trees.

ENEMIES: Cabbage and strawberries are said by some companion gardeners to be poor companions, though others report no difficulties and even intercrop a new planting of berries with cabbage.

GROWING GUIDELINES: Set crowns 1½ feet (45 cm) apart in beds or in rows 3 feet (90 cm) apart in light, well-drained soil in full sun. Mulch thickly with straw. Overcrowded beds invite disease; thin out crowded plantings to prevent problems. Most strawberry beds begin to decline after 3–4 years; start a new patch with fresh plants on a different site every 3 years to have a continuous supply of berries.

COMMENTS: June-bearers produce a single large crop and spread rapidly by runners. Ever-bearers produce a moderate main crop in June and a scattering of berries later in the summer; they are slower to fill in the bed.

Helianthus annuus   Compositae

SUNFLOWER

Research is turning up strong evidence of allelopathy in sunflowers. Just how significant the effect is in the home garden has yet to be determined.

ALLIES: None known.

COMPANIONS: Sunflowers are commonly planted with corn, beans, and squash. Plant a strip of tall-growing sunflowers between plantings of popcorn and sweet corn to block wind-borne pollen that could cross-pollinate the crops.

ENEMIES: Wild sunflowers, a common crop weed, have been shown to inhibit or prevent the growth of many species of plants. Field and laboratory studies show that cultivated types can be equally detrimental to some of their neighbors. Most home companion gardeners notice no detrimental effects from the plants; some claim that the sunflower hulls dropped from bird feeders inhibit plant growth around the base of the feeder.

GROWING GUIDELINES: Sunflowers couldn't be simpler to grow. They thrive in average soil in full sun. In spring, after danger of frost has passed, push a seed ½ inch (12 mm) deep into the soil every 6 inches (15 cm); thin to 18–24 inches (45–60 cm) apart. You can transplant the thinnings. Plants are drought-tolerant, but mulching and regular watering will encourage larger seed heads.

COMMENTS: Before you cross sunflowers off your companion list, do a little experimenting yourself. Most research has been done on sunflower's effect on weeds, such as jimson weed, velvetleaf, Johnson grass, and others, not on home garden crops.

Tanacetum vulgare   Compositae

TANSY

Artemisia dracunculus   Compositae

TARRAGON

Companion gardeners recommend tansy to improve the vigor of roses and bramble fruits. The scent is also said to repel Japanese beetles, flea beetles, and many other pests.

ALLIES: Studies at Rodale's research farm in Pennsylvania indicated some reduction in numbers of squash bugs and Colorado potato beetles on crops interplanted with tansy, but researchers also noted an increase in imported cabbageworms.

COMPANIONS: Fast-growing tansy can quickly get out of hand in the loose, rich soil of the garden. Any benefits of companion planting tansy with other crops could be canceled out by the overcrowding effect of the tansy. If you want to grow tansy with other crops, consider planting it in a bottomless bucket that you've sunk into the soil.

ENEMIES: Research indicates that tansy may negatively affect collards.

GROWING GUIDELINES: Start from nursery plants or seed sown shallowly indoors or outdoors in spring. Grow in average, well-drained soil in full sun. Tansy grows and spreads very fast, even in poor soil; confine it in a border, a separate bed, or a wooden half-barrel. Divide overgrown plants in spring or fall.

COMMENTS: The yellow, button-like flowers attract butterflies and insects to the garden, including beneficials and predators as well as white cabbage moths. Tansy was formerly popular in herbalists' remedies, but its use can cause violent reactions and death. A toxin called thujone is the culprit; it is also found in wormwood.

Two tarragons are commonly sold: Russian and French. Rub a leaf and sniff before you buy; the eye-opening licorice scent (and flavor) is evident only in the French type.

ALLIES: Tarragon is one of the aromatic herbs recommended by companion gardeners to improve growth and flavor of neighboring vegetables.

COMPANIONS: Place a tarragon plant at the corners of raised beds, grow it in the herb garden, or interplant it among plots of tomatoes, potatoes, and other vegetables. Tarragon also adapts well to life in a container, either outside or on a sunny windowsill.

ENEMIES: None known. Tarragon is a member of the same genus as wormwood, but it appears to lack the toxic qualities of that herb.

GROWING GUIDELINES: Transplant purchased young plants 12–24 inches (30–60 cm) apart into well-drained, light, nonacid soil, in full sun. Make sure the plant gets good air circulation. Eight weeks after setting the plant out, cut stems back by about half. Pinch budding stems to keep plant vigorous. Divide older plants every 3 years in spring.

COMMENTS: Russian tarragon is a lanky plant with none of the signature licorice fragrance of the true French tarragon. French tarragon (the variety *sativa*) is obtainable only in pots. Russian tarragon is what you'll get if you grow plants from seed.

Freeze leaves in zippered plastic bags, or use fresh to flavor fish, chicken, cream soups, and other dishes. Use sparingly—the flavor of this herb is very strong and can overpower other ingredients.

| Thymus spp. | Labiatae | Lycopersicon esculentum | Solanaceae |

THYME

Delicately pretty in leaf and flower, a carpet of thyme makes a beautiful underplanting for roses. For extra interest, try silver thyme (Thymus x citriodorus 'Argenteus').

ALLIES: Companion gardeners recommend planting thyme with just about everything in the garden; this herb is said to improve flavor and repel pests. Eggplants, cabbage, potatoes, and tomatoes are often mentioned as companions. Scientific evidence is sparse; in one study, the presence of thyme appeared to increase the population of cabbageworms on neighboring plants. Another study suggests that thyme sprays may be more effective at masking plants from pests that seek hosts by smell. (See "Herbal Sprays" on page 86 for directions for making your own sprays.)

COMPANIONS: Grow only nonspreading types of this herb in the vegetable garden. Common thyme (*Thymus vulgaris*), an upright, shrubby type, is a good choice for interplanting with vegetables. Spreading, mat-forming thymes, such as the popular woolly thyme (*T. pseudolanuginosus*), are best kept in separate beds or in the herb and flower garden.

ENEMIES: None known.

GROWING GUIDELINES: Thyme thrives in poor to average, well-drained soil in full sun. Common thyme is easy to grow from seed sown shallowly indoors in late winter. Sprinkle the seed generously into pots. Buy other species and cultivars as plants from garden centers.

COMMENTS: Cuttings are extremely easy to root. Divide older plants in spring.

TOMATO

Companion gardeners plant tomatoes with asparagus, basil, broccoli, cauliflower, cabbages, carrots, onions, parsley, and sage, hoping for improved growth and flavor.

ALLIES: Dill and borage are said to deter hornworms. The weed spiny amaranth (*Amaranth spinosus*), a common garden invader, has lured black cutworms away from tomatoes in one study. In another study, intercropping tomatoes with plants of the cabbage family resulted in reduced populations of diamondback moths and flea beetles in cabbage-family crops.

Gardeners often interplant marigolds with tomatoes to control nematodes, but studies indicate that the best way to control nematodes—if they are indeed a problem in your garden—is to plant a whole bed of marigolds, then turn it under and follow it with tomatoes. Researchers in Rhodesia, where the marigold *Tagetes minuta* is a common weed, successfully controlled five species of nematodes by planting a whole crop of the marigold; tomatoes grown after the marigolds had a much-reduced number of root knots. Similar studies in India gave similar results: When tomatoes followed a planting of *T. erecta*, there were considerably less roots with knots, and the tomatoes were heavier.

COMPANIONS: Surround tomatoes with aromatic herbs, or plant them into an already-growing bed of spinach, lettuce, or other fast-growing crops.

ENEMIES: Black walnut roots cause tomato plants to wilt and die. See the Walnut, black entry on page 151 for more details on this allelopathy. Companion

TOMATO—Continued

TURNIP

To minimize the buildup of soilborne pests and diseases, avoid planting tomatoes where related plants, such as eggplants and potatoes, grew the previous year.

Turnips are generally problem-free but occasionally may be damaged by powdery mildew or leafminers. Destroy affected leaves; avoid overhead watering to prevent mildew.

gardeners believe that tomatoes fail to thrive when planted near fennel or potatoes.

GROWING GUIDELINES: Tomatoes thrive in full sun in deep, fertile, well-drained soil. Start plants from seed sown ¼ inch (6 mm) deep indoors, 5–6 weeks before the average date of the last expected frost in your area. Or buy nursery-grown plants. After all danger of frost has passed, set plants out in the garden; make the hole deep enough so soil covers the stem up to the bottom leaves. Space them 12–24 inches (30–60 cm) apart if you plan to cage or trellis the plants; allow 36–48 inches (90–120 cm) between plants if you plan to let them sprawl. Staked plants produce fewer tomatoes than those that are allowed to sprawl, but they are easier to pick. Mulch with compost in midsummer, and water once with fish emulsion when plants are in bloom.

COMMENTS: Most gardeners pick and destroy tomato hornworms when they spot them, but if you see white rice-like eggs on the green caterpillar, leave it alone. The eggs contain the larvae of parasitic wasps, which feed on the living caterpillar. By letting nature takes its course, you're increasing the population of the wasps.

ALLIES: Peas and turnips are good neighbors, according to companion gardeners.

COMPANIONS: In fertile soil, interplant turnips with slower-maturing cabbage-family crops, like brussels sprouts.

ENEMIES: Keep turnips away from potatoes, say companion gardeners.

GROWING GUIDELINES: Turnips grow fast, and they're frost-resistant. Plant in fertile, loose, well-drained soil in full sun. Direct-sow seed ½ inch (12 mm) deep, 4–6 weeks before the last spring frost. The small round seeds are difficult to sow with regular spacing; thin every few days after they sprout until the seedlings are 3 inches (7.5 cm) apart. Plant another crop in late summer for a fall harvest. For best flavor, water regularly, keeping soil moist.

COMMENTS: Like brussels sprouts and other members of the cabbage family, turnips taste sweeter after a touch of light frost. Turnip leaves are popular for greens, especially in the South. Pick the leaves when young and tender. Dig roots when they are 2–4 inches (5–10 cm) across. Boil and mash larger roots as you would potatoes; small roots are tender enough to eat whole.

Valeriana officinalis   Valerianaceae

VALERIAN

Companion gardeners probably plant valerian in the hope that its smell will be as repulsive to insects as it is to people! Cats and—supposedly—rats like the fetid smell.

ALLIES: Biodynamic gardeners, who follow the teachings of Rudolph Steiner, recommend valerian as "helpful" to vegetables and other plants, probably improving the growth and vigor.

COMPANIONS: This perennial herb, which can reach 5 feet (1.5 m) tall under cultivation, is best suited to the back of the herb garden.

ENEMIES: None known.

GROWING GUIDELINES: Valerian will grow in full sun or light shade and prefers rich, moist soil, although it tolerates less-than-ideal conditions. The seeds germinate erratically; it's usually best to start with a potted plant. In spring and fall, the plant sends out runners; sever young plants from the mother plant at the end of summer and transplant them elsewhere. Space plants 12 inches (30 cm) apart. Valerian has escaped gardens in this country and can be found along roadsides from Quebec to Minnesota, south to Ohio, Pennsylvania, and New Jersey.

COMMENTS: Valerian comes from the Latin word *valere,* meaning "to be strong," referring to the medicinal qualities of the herb. It has been prized for centuries as a tranquilizer, and drugs based upon the herb are still used today in some European countries.

Juglans nigra   Juglandaceae

WALNUT, BLACK

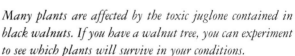

Many plants are affected by the toxic juglone contained in black walnuts. If you have a walnut tree, you can experiment to see which plants will survive in your conditions.

ALLIES: None known.

COMPANIONS: A few crops are known to be tolerant to varying degrees of the toxic juglone produced by these trees. If you can't move your garden or your tree, try these: beans, beets, grapes, onions, raspberries, and sweet corn. For ornamentals, gardeners suggest ajugas, bellflowers (*Campanula* spp.), alumroots (*Heuchera* spp.), daylilies, hostas, lily-of-the-valley, and sedums.

ENEMIES: The toxic juglone in walnut roots kills or stunts a long list of plants. Among the food crops, susceptible plants include alfalfa, blueberries, blackberries, peas, peppers, potatoes, and tomatoes. Ornamentals that often succumb or sicken include azaleas and rhododendrons (*Rhododendron* spp.), lilacs, magnolias, mountain laurel (*Kalmia latifolia*), and peonies. Raised beds that are 1–2 feet (30–60 cm) deep may help keep shallow-rooted plants out of harm's way. Container gardening is another alternative.

GROWING GUIDELINES: Plant young dormant trees in spring in full sun to partial shade. Black walnut trees thrive in deep, rich, moist soil.

COMMENTS: Black walnut trees produce heavy crops of tasty nuts, tough to crack but good for eating. The nuts are also relished by foraging squirrels—watch for plants springing up from nuts that forgetful squirrels buried in your garden.

Triticum vulgare   Gramineae

WHEAT

Avoid planting wheat near rye or barberry bushes. Barberries are a host plant in the life cycle of black stem rust, a wheat disease; rye may inhibit wheat growth.

ALLIES: None known.

COMPANIONS: Wheat thrives in a bed where peas, beans, clovers, and other legumes grew the previous season.

ENEMIES: Studies of the growth of lettuce seedlings in fields where cover crops (including wheat) had been incorporated showed a toxic effect on lettuce roots. When lettuce roots came close to or touched decaying debris, root tips browned and the plants were stunted. Toxins apparently leach from wheat if the plants are used as mulch or plowed under. In some studies, a mulch of wheat straw inhibited the germination of corn, reducing the rate by nearly half.

GROWING GUIDELINES: Broadcast seed by hand or with a crank-type spreader into a prepared seedbed with average, well-drained soil in full sun. Sow spring wheat about the time of the last spring frost date for a summer crop; sow winter wheat around the first frost date in fall for an early summer crop. Sow about 4 pounds (8 kg) of seed per 1,000 square feet (93 sq m). Harvest when kernels can be dented but not squashed with a fingernail.

COMMENTS: To remove the chaff, winnow wheat on a windy day. Slowly pour the kernels from one container to another, letting the wind blow the chaff away. For small amounts of homegrown flour, use a blender to mill the kernels.

Artemisia absinthium   Compositae

WORMWOOD

Wormwood is a large perennial herb with gray-green leaves and a strong scent. Keep it clipped back for dense growth; use the clippings for insecticidal and repellent sprays.

ALLIES: None known.

COMPANIONS: Wormwood is a pretty plant, despite its unappealing name. Use it in ornamental plantings or as an attractive, silvery hedge, but keep vegetable plants away.

ENEMIES: Companion gardeners note that few plants thrive when planted near wormwood. Glandular hairs on the surface of the leaves produce volatile oils and the inhibiting toxin absinthin. Rain or overhead watering washes the substances from leaves, and this will poison nearby plants. One scientist experimented with wormwood leaves, digging them into the soil. This retarded or reduced the germination of peas and beans and stunted the bean plants that did manage to sprout.

GROWING GUIDELINES: Sow the small seeds shallowly in pots in spring, or start with nursery-grown plants. Set plants into a permanent bed in average, well-drained soil in full sun. Wormwood self-sows moderately if left to go to seed. Low-growing branches will root wherever they touch soil. Take cuttings or divide overgrown clumps in early spring or early fall.

COMMENTS: Try a wormwood spray on flea beetles, cabbageworms, and other pests (see "Herbal Sprays" on page 86 for directions). Use dried leaves in sachets to repel clothes moths.

Achillea spp.	Compositae	*Zinnia elegans*	Compositae

YARROW

ZINNIA

Yarrow bears flat flower clusters that attract insects, including many beneficials. The ferny foliage provides good cover for lady beetles and other predaceous species.

Interplant zinnias in the vegetable garden to add a dash of color. Butterflies and beneficial insects are drawn by the flowers; birds often appreciate the seeds.

ALLIES: Biodynamic gardeners, who follow the teachings of Rudolph Steiner, believe that yarrow increases the oil content of aromatic herbs.

COMPANIONS: This airy, delicate-looking plant spreads fast in loose, rich garden soil and self-sows abundantly. Plant in ornamental beds and the herb garden. In the vegetable garden, deadhead vigilantly and use barriers to contain its growth. Plant creeping, low-growing types as fragrant groundcovers around garden benches, where foot traffic is light.

ENEMIES: None known.

GROWING GUIDELINES: Yarrow is easy to grow from seed. In early spring, sow shallowly in pots indoors to keep track of the tiny seedlings. Plant in average, well-drained soil in full sun when seedlings reach a manageable size. Divide large clumps in spring and fall to extend the planting.

COMMENTS: Yarrow blooms dry well for craft use; hang the flowers to dry and mix their pastel colors in wreaths and other crafts. The white-flowered American wildflower known as yarrow (*A. millefolium*) is actually a European import now naturalized in the U.S. Yarrow was once used in witches' incantations and for more pedestrian purposes such as staunching nosebleeds and healing sores.

ALLIES: Zinnias attract insects of all kinds to the garden with their bright flowers and bushy foliage. Nectar-seeking wasps and hover flies are two of the beneficials that come to the feast. Zinnias also attract butterflies of many species, from small coppery metalmarks to big, showy swallowtails.

COMPANIONS: Zinnias are outstanding plants for beds, borders, and containers. These rewarding, gaily colored annuals bloom prolifically from summer until frost. Interplant in the vegetable garden to add a dash of color. Be sure to grow a few rows just for cutting; cut flowers stay fresh for over a week with no special treatment.

ENEMIES: None known.

GROWING GUIDELINES: Zinnas thrive in full sun in average, well-drained soil and are at their best in hot summer weather. They are among the quickest and easiest annuals you can grow from seed. Direct-sow $1/4$ inch (6 mm) deep in spring after danger of frost has passed. Deadhead regularly to keep the flowers coming. Powdery mildew often causes dusty white spots on the foliage. Antidessicant sprays may help protect leaves. Or look for resistant species and cultivars, such as *Zinnia angustifolia*.

COMMENTS: Let some plants go to seed to attract goldfinches and other seed eaters to the garden. Easy-to-grow zinnias are a great way to introduce children to the pleasures of growing flowers.

USDA

PLANT HARDINESS ZONE MAP

The map that follows shows the United States and Canada divided into 10 zones. Each zone is based on a 10°F (5.6°C) difference in average annual minimum temperature. Some areas are considered too high in elevation for plant cultivation and so are not assigned to any zone. There are also island zones that are warmer or cooler than surrounding areas because of differences in elevation; they have been given a zone different from the surrounding areas. Many large urban areas are in a warmer zone than the surrounding land.

Plants grow best within an optimum range of temperatures. The range may be wide for some species and narrow for others. Plants also differ in their ability to survive frost and in their sun or shade requirements.

The zone ratings indicate conditions where designated plants will grow well and not merely survive. Refer to the map to find out which zone you are in. In the "Plant by Plant Guide," starting on page 95, you'll find recommendations for the plants that grow best in your zone.

Many plants may survive in zones warmer or colder than their recommended zone range. Remember that other factors, including wind, soil type, soil moisture and drainage capability, humidity, snow, and winter sunshine, may have a great effect on growth.

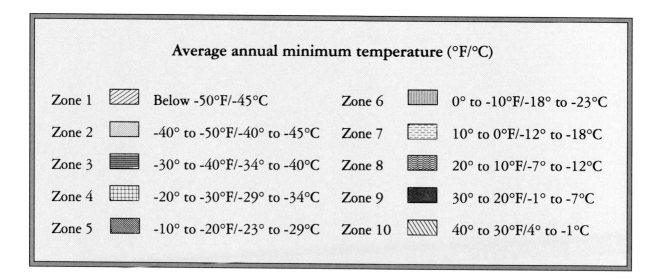

Average annual minimum temperature (°F/°C)

Zone 1		Below -50°F/-45°C	Zone 6		0° to -10°F/-18° to -23°C
Zone 2		-40° to -50°F/-40° to -45°C	Zone 7		10° to 0°F/-12° to -18°C
Zone 3		-30° to -40°F/-34° to -40°C	Zone 8		20° to 10°F/-7° to -12°C
Zone 4		-20° to -30°F/-29° to -34°C	Zone 9		30° to 20°F/-1° to -7°C
Zone 5		-10° to -20°F/-23° to -29°C	Zone 10		40° to 30°F/4° to -1°C

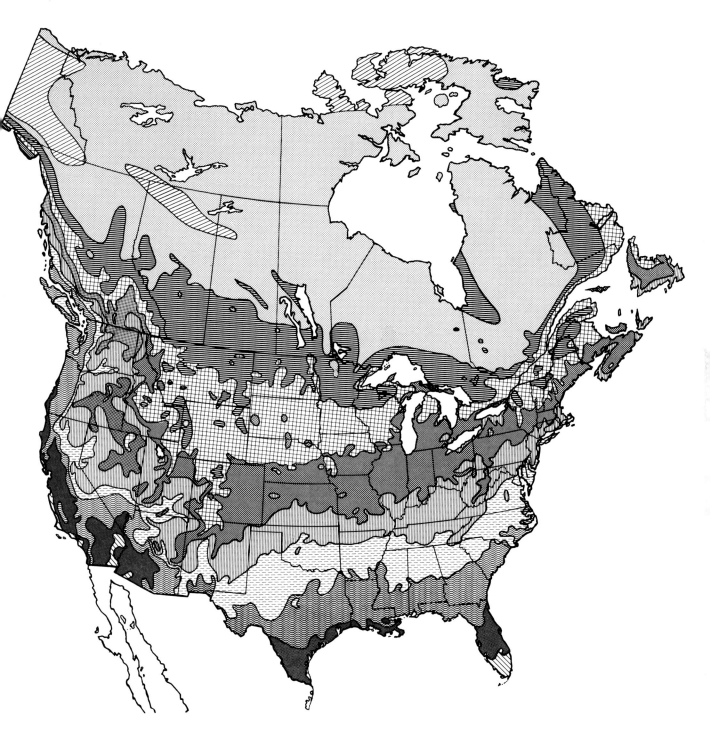

The numbers in bold indicate main entries, and the numbers in italic indicate illustrations.